Hg2 Buenos Aires

A Hedonist's guide to
Buenos Aires

Written and photographed by
Charles Froggatt

A Hedonist's guide to Buenos Aires

Managing director – Tremayne Carew Pole
Marketing director – Sara Townsend
Series editor – Catherine Blake
Design – Katy Platt
Maps – Andrew Thompson
Typesetting – Filmer Ltd
Printers – Printed in Italy by Printer Trento srl
Publisher – Filmer Ltd

Email – info@hg2.com
Website – www.hg2.com

First published in the United Kingdom in May 2007 by
Filmer Ltd
47 Filmer Road,
London SW6 7JJ

ISBN – 1-905428-08-1 / 978-1-905428-08-3

Hg2 Buenos Aires

CONTENTS

How to...

A Hedonist's guide to... is broken down into easy to use sections:
Sleep, Eat, Drink, Snack, Party, Culture, Shop, Play and Info. In each of
these sections you will find detailed reviews and photographs. At the
front of the book you will find an introduction to the city and an
overview map, followed by introductions to the four main areas and
more detailed maps. On each of these maps you will see the places
that we have reviewed, laid out by section, highlighted on the map with
a symbol and a number. To find out about a particular place simply turn
to the relevant section, where all entries are listed alphabetically.
Alternatively, browse through a specific section (e.g. Eat) until you find
a restaurant that you like the look of. Next to your choice will be a
small coloured dot – each colour refers to a particular area of the city.
Simply turn to the relevant map to discover the location.

Updates

Hg2 has developed a network of journalists in each city to review the
best hotels, restaurants, bars, clubs, etc., and to keep track of the latest
developments – new places open up all the time, while others simply
fade away or just go out of style. To access our free updates as well as
the content of each guide, simply log on to our website www.hg2.com
and register. We welcome your help. If you have any comments or
recommendations, please feel free to email us at info@hg2.com.

Book your hotel on Hg2.com

We believe that the key to a great city break is choosing the right
hotel. Our unique site now enables you to browse through our selection of hotels, using the interactive maps to give you a good feel for

the area as well as the nearby restaurants, bars, sights, etc., before you book. Hg2 has formed partnerships with the hotels featured in our guide to bring them to readers at the lowest possible price. Our site now incorporates special offers from selected hotels, as well as a diary of interesting events taking place, 'Inspire Me'.

The concept

A Hedonist's guide to… is designed to appeal to a more urbane and stylish traveller. The kind of traveller who is interested in gourmet food, elegant hotels and seriously chic bars – the traveller who feels the need to explore, shop and pamper themselves away from the crowds.

Our aim is to give you an insider's knowledge of a city, to make you feel like a well-heeled, sophisticated local and to take you to the most fashionable places in town to rub shoulders with the local glitterati.

In today's world work rules our life, and weekends away are few and far between; when we do manage to get away we want to have as much fun and to relax as much as possible with the minimum amount of stress. This guide is all about maximizing time. There is a photograph of each place we feature, so before you go you know exactly what you are getting into; choose a restaurant or bar that suits you and your needs.

We pride ourselves on our independence and our integrity. We eat in all the restaurants, drink in all the bars and go wild in the nightclubs – all totally incognito. We charge no one for the privilege of appearing in the guide, and every place is reviewed and included at our discretion.

We feel cities are best enjoyed by soaking up the atmosphere: wander the streets, indulge in some retail therapy, re-energize yourself with a massage and then get ready to eat like a king and party hard on the local scene.

Buenos Aires

You could confidently compare Buenos Aires to any city in the world and not find it wanting in any department. They say New York is a city where you can do anything, at any time of the day. This is probably the case with Buenos Aires, but the difference is that when Buenos Aires erupts, there is no other city like it.

Buenos Aires is the tenth largest city in the world, with three times more shrinks per capita than any other, arguably the best-looking people, almost as many plastic surgeons as found in Los Angeles, a population of *porteños* ('people from the port') who dance before going to work in the morning, and a culture of brick-thowing when football referees 'misbehave'.

It might be fair to say that *porteños* are ever so slightly '*loco!*'. But that's exactly why you'll love them.

Bars, nightclubs, strip clubs – yes, for girls too – after-hours clubs, and endless shopping are only part of this city's armoury. A hotel industry beginning to find an identity, which seems to have embraced 'urban

minimalism', and a restaurant trade adapting to a demand for alternatives to its incredible beef, mean the dynamism in BA has made it the continent's must-visit city.

Since the devaluation of the Argentine peso against the US dollar in January 2002, there has been a 70% drop in the value of the currency, but equally there's been a 70% rise in visitors coming to Buenos Aires, and tourism is now ranked alongside the country's exports as a principal source of revenue.

Argentina is also the eighth largest country in the world, which means the majority of visitors to Buenos Aires don't spend their entire trip here, but head out to explore this relatively untapped wilderness. Argentina boasts the world's southernmost city, huge waterfalls, the continent's only advancing glaciers, ski slopes, beaches, golf courses, polo clubs and the widest river estuary on the planet. In this guide we have covered almost all of the activities on offer throughout the country, as well as discovering some of the best hotels and, of course, the Uruguayan beach resort of Punta del Este, which brims with Argentine party animals and beach beauties from the end of December to February.

Get some sleep before you arrive in BA, remember to leave room in your luggage for shopping and prepare to be exposed to a world of limitless hedonism in a country where it costs little to play hard.

NÚNE

BELGRAN(

VILLA DEL
PARQUE

Av. Circunvalación Gral Paz

BUENOS

VILLA
REAL

AIRES

FLORES

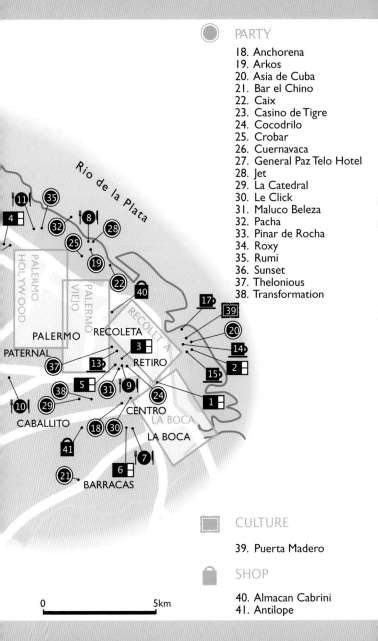

Buenos Aires city map

PARTY

18. Anchorena
19. Arkos
20. Asia de Cuba
21. Bar el Chino
22. Caix
23. Casino de Tigre
24. Cocodrilo
25. Crobar
26. Cuernavaca
27. General Paz Telo Hotel
28. Jet
29. La Catedral
30. Le Click
31. Maluco Beleza
32. Pacha
33. Pinar de Rocha
34. Roxy
35. Rumi
36. Sunset
37. Thelonious
38. Transformation

CULTURE

39. Puerta Madero

SHOP

40. Almacan Cabrini
41. Antilope

Rio de la Plata

PALERMO HOLLYWOOD
PALERMO VIEJO
PALERMO
PATERNAL
RECOLETA
RETIRO
CENTRO
CABALLITO
LA BOCA
BARRACAS

0   5km

Recoleta, Retiro and Palermo

If Palermo Viejo is style city and La Boca is tango central, then Recoleta is the 'dollars-under-the-mattress', 'anyone-for-tea?' part of town.

Unquestionably the most affluent, European zone of Buenos Aires, a fact that is mirrored by the stunning French architecture housing beautifully pampered residents, this is where the majority of the city's luxury hotel accommodation is to be found. Although lacking the *onda* (vibe) of the boutique hotels in Palermo Viejo and recent chic hotel openings to the centre, the best part of Recoleta – the area boxed in between Avenidas 9 de Julio, Las Heras, Pueyrredon and Libertador – is where you want to book your hotel room. Why? Well, first of all this area is the safest in Buenos Aires; second, the central location means that all *barrios* of the city are easy to reach; and third, it is the best-

maintained area, despite the surprises pampered pets leave for pedestrians on the street.

Bolivian, Paraguayan or Peruvian maids will pop out of old French apartment buildings to hand the Labrador over to the dog walker, while young Argentines strut past, ice-cream in one hand, cell phone in the other, gabbling on about which house in Punta del Este to take on in the summer. Doormen line the streets, sweeping up the dust picked up by the designer shoes of the residents, and young businessmen, flowers under their arm, march past on their way to meet their girlfriend's parents. Recoleta encapsulates Buenos Aires life at its most elegant.

To the east of Recoleta is Retiro, an area focused around Plaza San Martin, where jacaranda trees blossom from October to November. The plaza is overlooked by the Kavanagh Building, which was the highest in South America when built in 1935. While Recoleta's main

attraction has to be its cemetery (see Culture), Retiro is an important part of the city because of its British-built railway station, while its monuments – such as the Malvinas Memorial (see Culture) – are also important. For art fanatics, Arroyo street is impressive, while the Sofitel (see Sleep) is an extremely civilized place to stay.

To the west of Recoleta is the start of the *barrio* Palermo, another wealthy residential part of town, the largest in the city but without the abundance of French architecture to match Recoleta's elegance. Hedonistically speaking, Palermo's Alto Palermo shopping centre (see Shop) and the Spanish restaurant Oviedo (see Eat) are the highlights of this area, although the vast parks along Avenida del Libertador give the *porteños* a rural grounding among the speeding traffic.

0 — 500m

M Metro Station

Recoleta, Retiro & Palermo local map

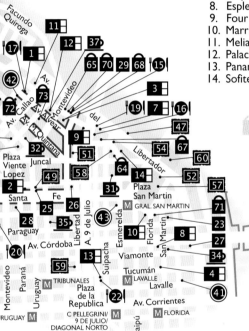

La Boca and San Telmo

Time travel does exist in Argentina. Europeans arrived on boats, adapted their way of life and became *porteños* (people from the port). La Boca and San Telmo tell the story of this development and are the only time capsules in Buenos Aires where life doesn't appear to have changed one bit. The *barrios* (neighbourhoods) lie side by side, south of Plaza de Mayo and east of Puerto Madero's revamped docklands, and are now, quite understandably, a focal point for tourists.

La Boca, an area flanked by the mouth (*boca*) of the river, is characterized by the tango, multicoloured buildings (on El Caminito) and football. Although the dance was originally developed in the suburbs of Buenos Aires, La Boca is the world centre; sadly, however, it has now become such a tourist attraction that shows and dancing lessons are better in other areas of the city (see Party). La Boca is not the kind of place you go for a midnight stroll, but its portside buildings look timeless when the light hits the coloured façades in the morning before the tour buses arrive. This is also the place where Diego Maradona, the legend whose talent surpassed even Pelé's in the eyes of every Argentine, played for Boca Juniors, a team you must go and watch at their beloved La Bombonera stadium.

San Telmo is a slightly safer neighbourhood than La Boca, and houses many of the city's backpacker hostels and larger, cheaper flats inhabited by bohemian *porteños* keen on turning old buildings into their private nightclubs. Named after Catholic priest Pedro Gonzalez Telmo, San Telmo is a maze of cobbled streets and crumbling mansions that once housed the city's wealthiest families before the cholera and yellow fever outbreaks in the late 19th century. Buenos Aires, arguably, would not be the architectural jewel it is without San Telmo's input. The hugely popular weekend antiques fair, Feria de Antiguedades, is held in Plaza Dorrego, although if you really want a taste of San Telmo, arrive during the week, before you are gobbled up by snap-happy tourists bearing 'fannypacks'.

Charmingly – or rather, alarmingly – both areas appear to be tumbling down. A few regeneration projects are currently under way to restore San Telmo in particular to its former glory. This is a neighbourhood living in the past, which is why San Telmo should take up at least a morning of your time in Buenos Aires. La Boca is a genuinely poor neighbourhood, and, to be honest, you only need to spend a couple of hours here to be satisfied you have seen everything.

Buenos Aires is now a cosmopolitan city, and these two historic neighbourhoods, though rough around the edges, carry enormous significance in terms of Buenos Aires' cultural identity.

SLEEP

1. 562 Nogaro
2. Mansión Vitraux
3. The Cocker

EAT

4. Brasserie Petanque
5. La Brigada
6. Patagonia Sur

DRINK

7. 647
8. Bar Dorrego
9. Buda Bar
10. Gibraltar

SNACK

11. El Desnivel
12. El Obrero

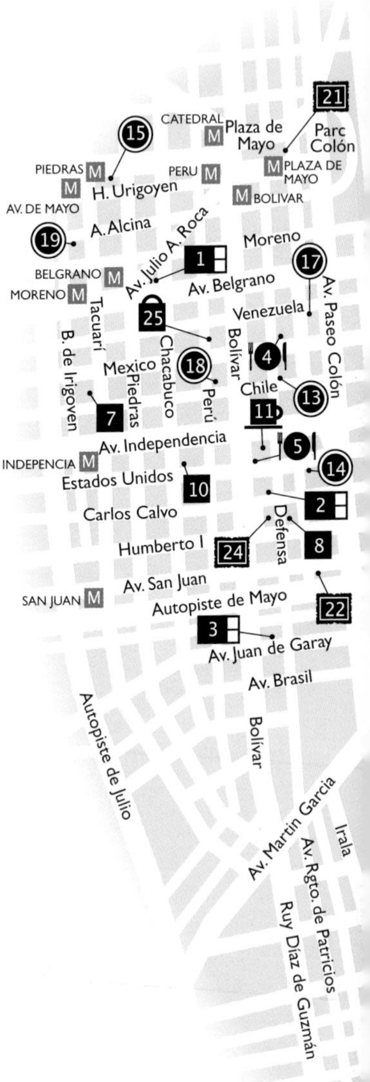

CATEDRAL
Plaza de Mayo
Parc Colón
PIEDRAS
PERU
PLAZA DE MAYO
H. Urigoyen
BOLIVAR
AV. DE MAYO
A. Alcina
Av. Julio A. Roca
Moreno
BELGRANO
MORENO
Av. Belgrano
Venezuela
Av. Paseo Colón
Tacuarí
B. de Irigoyen
Chacabuco
Bolívar
Mexico
Piedras
Perú
Chile
Av. Independencia
INDEPENCIA
Estados Unidos
Carlos Calvo
Defensa
Humberto I
Av. San Juan
SAN JUAN
Autopiste de Mayo
Av. Juan de Garay
Av. Brasil
Autopiste de Julio
Bolívar
Av. Martin Garcia
Irala
Av. Rgto. de Patricios
Ruy Díaz de Guzmán
21
15
19
1
17
25
4
18
13
7
11
5
14
10
2
24
8
22
3

La Boca and San Telmo local map

PARTY

13. Bar Seddon
14. Bar Sur
15. Café Tortoni
16. Casino Flotante de Buenos Aires
17. La Trastienda
18. Museum
19. Palacio Alsina

CULTURE

20. La Boca
21. La Casa Rosada & Plaza de Mayo
22. MAMBA
23. Museo de Bellas Artes de la Boca
24. Plaza Dorrego

SHOP

25. Pablo Ramirez

0   500m

M Metro Station

Palermo Viejo, Palermo Chico and Villa Crespo

You could spend two weeks in this part of Palermo without surfacing for air, although the lack of ATM machines would eventually mean you'd have to take an hour off before diving straight back into what has become BA's nocturnal party zone.

The important thing to realize is that Palermo Viejo and its immediate vicinity are where you will spend much of your time in Buenos Aires. The name is derived from the Franciscan abbey of Saint Benedict of Palermo (Saint Benedict the Moor), who lived from 1526 to 1589 and is a patron saint of Palermo in Sicily, whence many immigrants came in the late 19th century. It spans over 174 square kilometres, making it the largest *barrio* in Buenos Aires. Latterly more famous than Saint Benedict was Che Guevara, who lived here, as did Jorge Luis Borges, Argentina's most famous author.

Argentines will be Argentines, however, and Palermo is now unofficially divided into smaller areas, which, to their credit, do actually help when you're pinpointing where to meet for a drink, a shop or dinner.

The map for this area (see overleaf) predominately covers Palermo Viejo (Old Palermo) but also includes the bordering Palermo Chico (Small Palermo) and Villa Crespo areas.

Strictly speaking, Palermo Viejo – slightly older than the surrounding areas – is boxed in by Avenidas Santa Fe, Scalabrini Oriz, Córdoba and Juan B. Justo, while Villa Crespo lies west of Córdoba on the map and Palermo Chico is east of Santa Fe. Within Palermo Viejo is an area known as Palermo Soho, renamed in an attempt to make the trendiest blocks that border Juan B. Justo sound more exclusive. Plazoleta Cortázar (unofficially known as Plaza Serrano) is the central point of

Palermo Soho, where hippy markets and art fairs take place at weekends.

It's all more than a little confusing, but *porteños* will be impressed if you know the difference between Chico, Hollywood, Soho and Viejo.

The area centred on Plaza Palermo Viejo has exploded with life in the last decade: houses once used as mechanics' workshops have become chic boutique hotels, old meat shacks have become cutting-edge fashion outlets and ex-cobblers have become Martini-sipping wateringholes, although the artisanal and bohemian edge lingers on.

With height restrictions on the buildings, Palermo Viejo is sensibly low-rise and in part the streets are still cobbled. The roads are flanked by 'hole-in-the-wall' *asado* eateries juxtaposed with elegant lingerie stores. Many of the houses have now been bought or rented by young designers and the like, but still the odd family who seem to have been caught in a time-warp for 50 years linger on, making a striking visual contrast with Buenos Aires' young, affluent and attractive citizens buzzing around with shopping bags in hand, nodding away to the sounds of their iPods.

Palermo Viejo is an area on the move in Buenos Aires – an example of this city's ever-changing culture – and it could make or break your stay here.

As for the neighbouring Villa Crespo, it's on the grittier side of Córdoba and, despite the presence of the highly rated bar 878 (see Drink), and one of our favourite restaurants, Thymus (see Eat), the area has a way to go.

Palermo Chico, which ends at Avenida Sarmiento, is one of the more affluent residential areas in the city and includes two wonderful restaurants, Guido's Bar and Lucky Luciano (see Eat), owned by father and son respectively.

SLEEP

1. Bobo
2. Costa Petit

0   500m

M   Metro Station

EAT

3. Bar Uriarte
4. Bereber
5. Desde el Alma
6. Guido's
7. La Cabrera
8. Little Rose
9. Lucky Luciano
10. Thymus

DRINK

11. 878
12. Casa Cruz
13. Congo
14. El Diamante
15. Kim y Novak
16. Mott
17. Mundo Bizarro
18. Tazz

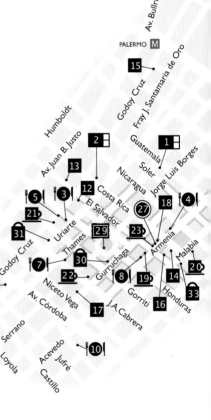

Palermo Hollywood & Las Cañitas

North of Juan B. Justo lies Palermo Hollywood, which, strictly speaking is part of Palermo Viejo but was renamed owing to the plethora of media companies in the area. Today, Hollywood is a darker, edgier and more playful *barrio* than its Palermo Viejo neighbour.

Gastronomically speaking, the area is home to Buenos Aires' less traditional restaurants, essentially meaning there is less beef on the menu: principally, there's the Peruvian-Japanese fusion Osaka, and South East Asian restaurants Green Bamboo and Sudestada (see Eat).

Although not a part of town for sightseeing, Palermo Hollywood is beginning to attract more boutique shops, and the row of bars on Honduras Street is growing daily. The most influential addition to the area came with the opening of Home Hotel (see Sleep), which has to be one of the top boutique hotels. Do also consider Sunday brunch at Olsen (see Eat) and a visit to Lobby wine bar (see Drink). There are more hotels under construction in the area, so check our website for updates.

North of Palermo Hollywood, facing the race track and nestled behind the Campo Argentino de Polo, where the jaw-dropping Argentine Open is played during November and December (see PLAY), is Las Cañitas, a former slum but now home to a strip of bars and restaurants on Baez street that attracts drinkers from Palermo's various enclaves and neighbouring Belgrano.

Las Cañitas is home to various boutique shops, most notably Rapsodia (see Shop), which has, in the minds of most Argentine men, revolutionized the way women wear jeans. Although the area is always busy in the evenings, there is the slightest hint that this area is now a little passé. In-the-know, snobby Argentines will tell you that the difference between Las Cañitas in 2003 and Las Cañitas today boils down to the number of *chetos* (nouveau riche) and *togas* (slang for *gatos*, the 'bridge and tunnel' element) that turn up and strip the area of its finesse. While this may be true, it doesn't matter – Las Cañitas is an amusing initiation into Buenos Aires' punishing nightlife, particularly during the week, when bars such as Kandi (see Drink) fill to bursting with hundreds of young divas.

To the north-west of Las Cañitas and Palermo Hollywood is Belgrano (not on the map), which is a quieter area of the city but nevertheless useful for unwinding: seek out My BA Hotel (see Sleep) and one of our favourite bars, Puerta Uno (see Drink).

PARTY

17. Ink
18. La Conzuelo
19. Niceto

SHOP

20. La Corte Vintage
21. Manifesto
22. Pasion Argentina
23. Rapsodia

```
0          500m
```

Ⓜ Metro Station

sleep...

In towns like Los Angeles and Miami, the hipper your hotel room key is, the more fashionable you are. In Buenos Aires, this is not the case: where you eat, which VIP room you burst your way into and how unaffected you are by *histericismo* (Buenos Aires 'mind games') are all far more important.

And there is a reason for this. Because of the massive rise in tourism in Argentina since the unpegging of peso from the US dollar in 2002, hotels in Buenos Aires are still able to charge 'hard currency' dollars without blinking, so it follows that most *porteños*, who still earn devalued pesos, are priced out of the hotel scene. You can therefore book any suite without worrying about your image in Buenos Aires being tarnished — not that you cared anyway, of course. Sleeping in Buenos Aires can be your own secret little adventure.

While we have included the best of the big hotels, much of our selection is boutique. As outsiders on the inside, we can tell you that while the larger hotel chains continue to deliver there has been an explosion of fabulous boutique hotels in Buenos Aires recently.

Of the larger hotels, the Palacio Duhau Park Hyatt, the Four Seasons and the Sofitel are the pick of the bunch. All have excellent central locations in or around Recoleta, within easy reach of every part of the city. If you are, or have pretensions of being, rich and/or aristocratic, high-society Argentines will intimate you are 'supposed' to stay at the Alvear Palace. We'll leave that up to you.

The Panamericano, which sits beside the obelisk, and the Marriott Plaza, which faces Plaza San Martin, boast idyllic locations, but lack style and atmosphere.

Of the larger boutique hotels, the 725 Continental and the Esplendor — funky and minimalist, respectively — are two exceptionally designed hotels in the centre. The same goes for Design Suites and the Design CE, which neighbour each other in Recoleta. The development of the latter by the Design Suites' architect has caused quite a legal stir.

In the smaller boutique category, which is where it's at, Bobo and the pioneering Home hotel (below) have sent a frisson of excitement through the Palermo Viejo scene. Home, with its boutique chic, is one of our favourites, while the Costa Petit would be anyone's number one choice for a four-room slice of style in an atmospheric, cobbled street. For a 'naughty weekend' playboy bachelor pad, slightly rough around the edges, consider Palermo 1551.

Meanwhile, down in San Telmo, the Cocker deserves the accolade of the finest hotel in the area, while the Mansión Vitraux is a stylish alternative for a different breed of tango enthusiast.

If you're looking for more of a stylish guesthouse in a happening area, then Krista in Palermo Hollywood ticks all the boxes. If your body and soul require a boutique getaway, then My BA Hotel in Belgrano will answer your prayers. For B&Bs, La Otra Orilla is charming. But for something a little different, look no further than the Youkali hotel.

The truth is that you will gain more respect by telling *porteños* that you are renting a flat in Buenos Aires. Argentines favour longer lasting relationships, whether it be for friendship or a fleeting romance, so like to hear you are in town to sample their culture over a period of time. The best piece of advice we can give you is to stay in Buenos Aires for as long as possible. Try Buenos Aires Habitat for temporary rentals: www.buenosaireshabitat.com (tel: 4815 8662).

Our top 10 places to stay in Buenos Aires are:
1. Palacio Duhau Park Hyatt
2. Home
3. Costa Petit
4. Four Seasons
5. Faena Hotel + Universe
6. The Cocker
7. Bobo
8. Alvear Palace Hotel
9. Esplendor
10. 725 Continental

Our top 5 for style are:
1. Faena Hotel + Universe
2. Palacio Duhau Park Hyatt
3. Home
4. Costa Petit
5. Mansión Vitraux

Our top 5 for location are:
1. Palacio Duhau Park Hyatt
2. Alvear Palace Hotel
3. Bobo
4. Panamericano
5. Home

Our top 5 for atmosphere are:
1. Faena Hotel + Universe
2. Home
3. Palacio Duhau Park Hyatt
4. Esplendor
5. Bobo

248 Finisterra, Báez 248 (1426), Las Cañitas
Tel: 4773 0901   www.248finisterra.com
Rates: US$105–179

Las Cañitas' first real boutique hotel, 248 sits right beside Soul Café (see Drink), the focal point of Báez's strip of bars. Entered through an inconspicuous street door, the hotel is housed in a low-rise, early 20th-century building with 11 rooms, a small wine bar on the ground floor and a sundeck with

stargazing Jacuzzi. All the rooms are cosy, with wooden floors, lime green walls, mini bars and freshly pressed white linen. Intimate and refreshing the hotel, while not exactly five-star luxury, is ideally placed and well equipped for a couple of days at the coal face. Massage and yoga are available either on deck or below, either before or after a couple of looseners in one of Báez's bars. They say Las Cañitas is slightly passé, but take the opening of 248 Finisterra as a sign that the trendsetters could return to stargaze once more in this neighbourhood. The polo ground is only a few yards away.

Style 7, Location 8, Atmosphere 8

562 Nogaro, Av Julio A. Roca 562, San Telmo
Tel: 4331 0091   www.562nogaro.com
Rates: US$130–190

There are three modern hotels with a boutique feel to them in the centre of town: our favourite, the Esplendor, the funky 725 Continental, and now 725's sister hotel, the 562 Nogaro. While not as slick as the other two and lacking somewhat in facilities (no bedside jacuzzis or rooftop pool), the 562 Nogaro 'does the job'. The refurbished four-star hotel, re-opened in late 2006, is located just a couple of blocks from Plaza de Mayo, the focal point around which Buenos Aires was built. Comfortable, independent, and in the bustling heart of the city, 562 is not about fashion or seeing and being

seen. Rather, the 562 Nogaro offers an uncomplicated, clean and modern place to sleep – remember this is the 725 Continental's sister hotel so quality is guaranteed – and a base from which to make your assault on San Telmo and the surrounding areas. It is only a 10-minute cab ride away from Recoleta if the traffic fumes become too intoxicating, and there are plenty of subway stations in this part of town.

Style 6, Location 8, Atmosphere 6

Alvear Palace Hotel, Avenida Alvear 1891, Recoleta

Tel: 4808 2100 www.alvearpalace.com
Rates: US$630–3,700

Refurbished in 1984, the Alvear, considered among Argentina's top social circles to be the only hotel in Buenos Aires, is the automatic choice for aristocrats, royalty and polo patrons here to spend a fortune on horses. Perfectly located on Avenida Alvear, the hotel is, of course, unnecessarily expensive. With a slightly musty smell, bold French carpets and a lobby full of scent and Swiss watch advertisements, you know you are paying for status, not chic-finesse. Think overstated elegance rather than decadent luxury. The hotel is spread over most of this Recoleta block. It's big, but to its credit you wouldn't know it when you walk in since it has been divided up into shopping centres, ballrooms and restaurants – Jean Paul Bondoux's La Bourgogne is excellent for dinner. Approach the doors and the *gendarme-*

lookalike bell-boys will rush for your bags before showing you to one of the 210 Louis XIV and Louis XVI styled rooms. The spaces are a mishmash of flowery upholstery with antiques in every corner, touch-screen telephones, flat-screen TVs and spa baths to go with the vintage gold taps. The penthouse, at over US$3,500 a night, includes a bed made for Shaquille O'Neil. At around 8 feet, they say you can fit at least six ESPN promotion girls on

it. Don't forget to look up the stunning spiral staircase (should you fancy some exercise, the current record for an ascent is a minute and a half).

Style 8, Location 9, Atmosphere 7

Bel Air, Arenales 1462, Recoleta

Tel: 4021 4000   www.hotelbelair.com.ar
Rates: AR$390–570

Ignore the Bel Air's claim that it is located in Barrio Norte: aside from La

Isla, this is as good an inner-Recoleta location as you will find. The hotel is tucked away on the better side of Callao, surrounded by antiques shops, designer boutiques and hair salons for professional housewives, and it's only a few yards from

Plaza Vicente Lopez, perhaps the most fashionable park for showing off one's pedigree poodle. At the Bel Air you are safe, and that is what you are paying upwards of 390 pesos for in this converted 1920s building, still handsomely dressed in its period white façade. Inside, judge the Bel Air on the cosy lobby, which features nicely pretentious space-age raised comfort booths overlooking the restaurant, with its views of Arenales street. Do not expect luxury: the rooms are stark, but nevertheless spacious and well lit. Ask for one of the top-floor suites, which have balconies facing the street, perfect for soaking up the atmosphere of this well-heeled neighbourhood. The Shamrock, El Alamo, Milión and El Gran Bar Danzon (see Drink) are all within walking distance. For an excellent dinner, pop out to Sirop or Resto.

Style 6, Location 8, Atmosphere 7

Bobo, Guatemala 4822, Palermo Viejo
Tel: 4774 0505 www.bobohotel.com
Rates: US$120–135

Bobo (standing for 'Bohemian Bourgeois') is indeed suited to the creative types among us, but the design is somewhat unique, since it's stylish and understated enough to attract both the insanely affluent urban traveller as well as the more bourgeois and humdrum visitor. In addition, Bobo's discreet Palermo Viejo location on Guatemala Street is just right for launching an assault on Buenos Aires' hip shopping, culinary and bar scene, all within walking distance. With a highly acclaimed restaurant and a young,

sexy vibe, this hotel only lacks a swimming pool. But you wouldn't come here to tread water anyway. On arrival, Belen, the manager, will escort you up to one of the seven rooms in the metallic warehouse lift. The rooms are simple, but spiced up with individual themes. The newspaper room, which sports 'tabloid paper' pillows and curtains, makes for interesting bedtime reading. The loft-styled penthouse boasts a Jacuzzi – with room for two – and a domino set. The hotel's price range and location attract young, affluent couples as well as the discerningly rich who like to stay under the radar.

Style 7, Location 9, Atmosphere 8

Caesar Park, Posadas 1086, Recoleta
Tel: 4819 1100   www.caesar-park.com
Rates: US$500–3,500

Serious businessmen enjoy being handed their print-outs by the stunning female staff at the Caesar's communications centre, while their wives – here for bargain leather shopping – spend a fortune in the Patio Bullrich shop-

ping centre, which conveniently sits in front of the hotel. As well as an assortment of smart European and South American visitors, the Caesar's 183 rooms are favoured by businessmen and politicians – including Brazilian presidents – because this hotel is slightly lower key (and less stylish) than the Four Seasons and the Palacio Duhau Park Hyatt. It does, however, still deserve its five-star status. The impressive entrance, soaring pillars and marble floors would make a fine cover shot for a glossy magazine, but at the same time it intimates a reluctance to really be a let-your-hair-down kind of establishment. With the odd gold tap and wooden finishes in the rooms and en-suites, an underground swimming pool and massage parlour, the Caesar is about prestige and comfort, not hell-raising fun – although you might be a little surprised to learn what some of these business folk get up to. The resident Agraz (see

35

Eat) restaurant deserves its high accolades and atracts a refined crowd.

Style 6, Location 8, Atmosphere 6

Claridge, Tucumán 535, Micro Centro

Tel: 4314 7700 www.claridge.com.ar
Rates: US$150–170

Padded walls and soundproofed windows go with elegant English design in
this banking district hotel. The Claridge is popular with besuited financiers
and locals loyal to the Piano Bar. All 153 rooms – some smaller than others
– live up to five-star expectations; the offices in the suites are 'carefully
placed separately from the bedrooms so that business does not turn into
pleasure' (which overlooks the well-stocked minibars). The lobby bar comes
highly acclaimed, and despite the built-up location, there is an outdoor pool.
Conveniently, the Claridge will store your luggage for you if you decide
you'd like to see a lot more of Argentina, but despite this it's not really the
best holiday-maker's choice; rather, it suits those in town on business who
are fond of classic hotels where nothing is left to chance (it even loans cell
phones to guests who need them while they're in town). The original bank

buildings in Buenos Aires are off the tourist trail, so take advantage of this
and make time to see the physical foundations of Argentina's economy. This
is a well-oiled hotel in a gritty area, but within easy reach of San Telmo.

Style 6/7, Location 5, Atmosphere 7

The Cocker, Avenida Juan de Garay 458, San Telmo
Tel: 4362 8451 www.thecocker.com
Rates: US$65–85

It took Ian and Aiden six months to oust the squatters of what was once a San Telmo slum, before they invested every penny they had on its reconstruction and redesign. The hotel is named after Rocco, their chirpy cocker spaniel, who sniffs guests up and down as they wander around the piano room, kitchen and sitting room. For those guests with allergic reactions to canines, rest assured that Rocco has not yet learned to scale the al fresco metallic staircase to the roof garden, where movies are projected onto the wall of the neighbouring building during the evenings. Pop downstairs for a glass of wine in the rustic wooden kitchen with Ian and  Aiden, where they'll describe the state this building was in when they found it – you'll be amazed. This seven room hotel is fit for the most stylish of guests. The Garden Suite is decked out with a four-poster bed over which a contemporary glass-walled bathroom is built. Meanwhile, the bed in room 26-02 is made out of the building's recycled staircase and 17-04 has a specially created 'conversation' pit piled with fur and cushions. With seven rooms from US$65 to US$85 per night, Ian and Aiden could charge at least double. But that's not their style. This is a quality piece of design soaked in a chilled, warm atmosphere. The rooms do not include televisions or radios, so think up some stimulating chat on the plane. If not, Ian and Aiden will eke something interesting out of you. The entrance is a small door beside a flower and vegetable shop on Avenida Juan de Garray. Your local is superstylish 647 (see Drink) and La Brigada (see Eat) is nearby for a steak.

Style 9, Location 6, Atmosphere 9

725 Continental, Avenida Roque Saenz Peña 725, Centre
Tel: 4131 8000   www.725continental.com
Rates: US$200–400

Crisply designed by Urgell-Penedo-Urgell in a refreshingly bling boutique style, the 725 Continental is the hip historian's choice. Located on Avenida Roque Saenz Peña between Buenos Aires' obelisk and pink presidential house, the hotel boasts a rooftop pool deck overlooking the old city domes. Formerly the Hotel Continental, built in 1927 by Alejandro Bustillo, this triangular French pile (situated where three streets meet, shaving off part of the block) quaintly mirrors New York's Flatiron building. Inside, or 'adentro' as they say in BA, the retro pop lounge lobby is also reminscent of the US –

Manhattan, Miami and Los Angeles. What was a crumbling relic of a hotel has provided Buenos Aires' central hotel industry with a stylish new 192-room facelift. The corner suites are rather overpriced, but you are paying for a central location, the roof deck and the reality that this (the 725's sister hotel is the 562) is the only design hotel in the area. The rooms all exude a sophisticated, minimalist feel and are strangely warmed by the mix of wood and metal fittings. It's invitingly hip, and the hotel's inconspicuous location close to Buenos Aires' historic sights is refreshing (while the city's more fashionable destinations remain but a taxi-ride away).

Style 8, Location 7, Atmosphere 8

Costa Petit, Costa Rica 5141, Palermo Viejo
Tel: 4776 8296/94   www.costapetithotel.com
Rates: US$150–$250

Stranger things have happened, but not many. A Palermo Viejo mechanic's workshop has become Buenos Aires' most stylish boutique hotel. What was

the spare parts shed is now an art deco super-suite, and what was the garage pit is now a turquoise pool overlooked by sculptures of angels. Designed and owned by carpenter Diego Padilla and interior designer Eugenia Choren – who styled the Rincón del Socorro Estancia in Los Esteros del Ibera – Costa Petit opened in late 2006, the product of the couple's passion for wood and fabrics. The result is a work of art. Diego's wood flooring and furniture is subtly complemented by Eugenia's use of soft textiles. Guests – mechanics included – can now rent the entire hotel for a mere US$800. But if you are willing to share, there are four rooms to go round. The heaviest wooden door in the province opens from the street into Costa Petit's library lobby and sitting room. This chill-zone room is just a metre away from the pool, which is a couple of metres away from the smoothly sophisticated rooms. The bar is a step away from the sofas that court the pool and Brazilian grass garden, overlooked too by the suites. This private haven in BA's most happening area is boutique-hotel heaven.

Style 9/10, Location 8, Atmosphere 8

Design CE, Marcelo T de Alvear 1695, Recoleta
Tel: 5237 3100   www.designce.com
Rates: US$140–260

The transparent glass floor in the back lobby hangs directly over the subterranean pool below, which gets the heart beating nicely before you head down past the pool itself to the basement bar; here, you stand suspended on industrial grid metal over the building's vast anti-fire water tanks. Floorless design from Ernesto Goransky, you could say. And the next-door Design Suites & Towers hotel (see below) has something else to add, along

the lines of 'to say we are a little angry is an understatement'. Having designed their hotel in 1999, seven years later Ernesto designed the Design CE along the same lines. The Design Suites & Towers have since filed a law-suit. But this is not your problem. The lawsuit may be born more out of envy than anything else, because Design CE is ever so slightly more stylish, taking the playful minimalist concept to another level with its downstairs amenities. The one-upmanship is across the board, with larger suites (56 square metres) and a pool that is – unlike its neighbour's – for swimming in. You cannot, however, squirt the hoses in the 'fireman's bar', which rejoices in the name of the 'Design Club'. Accommodation ranges from standard rooms with views of the dramatic Ministry of the Economy and Rodriguez Peña square, to the penthouse suite – a minimalist bunker loft with a balcony.

Style 8/9, Location 8, Atmosphere 8/9

Design Suites & Towers, Marcelo T de Alvear 1683 (between Rodriquez Peña and Montevideo), Recoleta
Tel: 4814 8700 www.designsuites.com
Rates: US$120–160

When Design Suites opened in 1999 it was the first real urban boutique hotel in Recoleta. Situated bang in front of the Palcio Pizzurno, which hous-es Argentina's Ministry of Education, it's essentially a new-age concept eyeing up a historic sight. The lobby 'mirage pool' will have you aching for a dip, but it's purely an aesthetic feature. Combined with a warming chill-out mix, it does, however, get guests ready for a night on the town. Think of this place

as the original contemporary minimalist hotel, with a faithful client list; it was designed by Ernesto Goransky before he designed the Design CE Hotel just up the block (see above). At 50 square metres, the suites are double the size of the standard rooms, so pay the extra $40 for your sitting room and view over the Plaza Rodriquez Peña. A youthful, party crowd, many of whom are European, drink around the pool; here they discuss the modern art that surrounds them and choose the bar to head to that night. The hotel has access to the local fitness centre's pool – don't go anywhere near it. Do, however, visit your local bars: Milión, El Alamo and Deep Blue (see Drink). Clásica y Moderna (Avenida Callao 892, tel: 4811 4812) is a block away for the tango enthusiast.

Style 7/8, Location 8, Atmosphere 8

Esplendor, San Martin 780, Micro Centro

Tel: 5256 8800   www.esplendorbuenosaires.com
Rates: US$155–232

Smell, hear and feel the bustle of Buenos Aires then retreat to this chic, minimalist haven. The dark horse of Buenos Aires' hotel design, the Esplendor is the converted Phoenix Hotel attached to the Galeria Pacifico shopping centre. The location is far from romantic – you are right at the city's Micro Centro coal face – but this historic building has an ice-cool heart, and the Esplendor is exactly the kind of hotel you want to return to

41

after a heavy night's clubbing. It feels clean and the stark spacious rooms will clear the head. The building's 20th-century white stone Italian façade con-

ceals three 60-square-metre penthouse suites with bedside Jacuzzis, twenty 40-square-metre suites and twenty eight 25-square-metre rooms; the doors to the rooms are over 4 metres high. All feature bold cement lines, ooze attitude and top Buenos Aires' league for stylish urban modernism. There is also an Esplendor Hotel down in El Calafate, a convenient base if you plan to visit Patagonia's famous Los Glaciares National Park. El Claustro Santa Catalina (see Snack) in front of the hotel is a peaceful spot for lunch.

Style 9, Location 5, Atmosphere 8

Faena Hotel + Universe, Martha Salotti 445, Puerto Madero
Tel: 4010 9000 www.faenahotelanduniverse.com
Rates: US$500–5,000

A must for lovers of kitsch. Breathtaking in parts and enjoyably over-the-top in others, this old red brick storehouse was gutted, rebuilt and redecorated by designer Philippe Starck. Set in the rapidly expanding docklands of Puerto Madero, the Faena Hotel + Universe does justice to its name, living in its own little world of catwalks, cabarets and anything glossy since Alan Faena – look out for the cowboy hat – opened the site in 2004. Undemiably luxuri-ous, one could easily spend a week here without leaving, so if you're looking for fashionable segregation in a slightly cut-off area close to touristy dock-side restaurants (which is what Puerto Madero really is), then the Faena delivers. The towering corridor entrance has that jaw-dropping Alice in

Wonderland feel to it, while the scarlet sun lounge and infinity pool deck is unmatched in Buenos Aires. The Faena's day spa attracts the city's most glamorous, so rest assured you won't just be bathing alongside pasty tourists; the menu offers every treatment and treat you imaginable, including a fabulous-ly luxuriant *hammam*. Each of the 105 rooms has white god-dess beds, red carpets and transparent glass-fronted bath-rooms, complemented by elec-

tric shutters, velvet curtains, flat-screen televisions and Dolby surround sound technology. Pop down to the all-white El Bistro restaurant, a hideous-ly grotesque but hugely entertaining room – the white plastic unicorn heads would also fit well in Garry Neville's breakfast salon. Each guest is assigned an experience manager, which is a wonderful touch, but, unfortunately, they are not wired into the Buenos Aires scene as much as we would like. Have a chat with one of the ready-to-play-at-Wimbledon waitresses instead.

Style 9, Location 5, Atmosphere 8

The Four Seasons, Posadas 1086, Recoleta
Tel: 4321 1200 www.fourseasons.com
Rates: US$420–6,500

The Buenos Aires branch of the Four Seasons chain is approaching urban hotel perfection. The Argentines have given this outfit a hint of sophistica-tion, while their Canadian godfathers have ensured it runs like clockwork – so much so that the only chink in the Four Seasons' armour is a slightly ropey surround sound system in the suites, although the minibars are impeccable. The building was taken over from the Hyatt in 2000 and a lavish refurbishment was completed in 2001; the end product will not fail to impress. Located at the posh end of Avenida 9 de Julio, the Four Seasons is armed with 138 rooms and 27 suites, seven of which are found in the Belle

Époque mansion built by Robert Prentice in 1916 for newlyweds Felix de Alzaga Unzue and Elena Peña. 'La Mansion' sits proudly behind the hotel's modern tower – where the 700-square-metre spa is housed – and swimming pool (one of the few outdoor pools in the city). The main façade of La Mansion is built in stone imported from Paris, while inside the musky scent of the vintage interior takes guests back to Buenos Aires' Belle Époque.

Now, almost a century after the Mansion's construction, the Rolling Stones, U2 and Argentina's favourite English son, Robbie Williams, have become regular guests when on tour, and royalty has also stayed here. The word in the elevators is that Mick Jagger prefers the modern tower, while Robbie likes the Mansion. So popular is the Four Seasons that during his 'Close Encounters' tour, Robbie could not get a room. He went to the Faena instead.

Style 9, Location 8, Atmosphere 8

Home, Honduras 5860, Palermo Viejo
Tel: 4778 1008 www.homebuenosaires.com
Rates: US$240–340

Englishman Tom Rixton – former record producer for Elastica and Simple Minds – made eye contact with Argentine blonde Patricia O'Shea in Dublin over a pint of the black stuff in 2001. They fell in love, married in 2002, moved to Buenos Aires and opened Palermo Viejo's Home hotel in 2005. They live happily ever after, and so do their guests, who now have to book well in advance. This kind of quality boutique hotel is pretty rare in Argentina. The 18 rooms and 3 separate penthouse suites, each clad in a different style of wallpaper (from flower-power to granny pad to Afghani poppy field), with sculpted bathrooms and rogue mini-bars (stocked by Tom himself), are enormously comfortable. Not unnecessarily luxurious, but comfortable – just as you would expect at home. The wild Brazilian grass garden features a delicious infinity pool and sunbathing deck, which is unheard of for a boutique hotel of this kind. The sub-terranean spa is pretty top-

of-the-range, while the cocktail bar is expertly manned and hosts DJ parties – thanks to Tom's long list of contacts – on a Friday evening.

Style 9, Location 9, Atmosphere 9

Hotel Emperador, Avenida del Libertador 420, Retiro
Tel: 4131 4000 www.hotelemperador.com.ar
Rates: US$180–600

Central and easy to get to, the Hotel Emperador claims to have the largest standard-size hotel rooms in Buenos Aires, at 41.5 square metres. Designed by Spaniards Rui Costa and Alvaro Vigil of the Arquiconcept Studio in Madrid and opened in 2000, the interior of this 265-room imperial tower is simultaneously intimidating and inviting. Head through the lobby past the platoon of semi-undercover guards to the creeper-enclosed garden for a drink, safe in the knowledge that your security will not be breached or your luggage stolen. If you are in town on business this could be right up your street. The Emperador is perched on Avenida del Libertador, 50 metres from the foot of Avenida 9 de Julio, supposedly the widest avenue in the world, and within sight of the Bank Boston tower; art buffs, too, will enjoy its situation parallel to Arroyo street, which is stuffed with excellent con-temporary art galleries. However, the hotel's five-star rating is a little bold: there is no spa to speak of, and the staff at the front desk are ever so slight-ly chippy, due in part to a regular stream of demanding clients during conference weeks. That said, Cecilia the PR girl is charming and the spacious, lilac coloured rooms flaunt their uninterrupted views of the River

Plate. Juana M is your hip Argentine basement restaurant right around the corner on Carlos Pelegrini, while Italian restaurant Piegari is the best of the under-the-motorway Recova eateries. For *gau-*

cho art, Marcos Bledel's gallery is also a 5-minute walk away on Cerrito.

Style 6, Location 8, Atmosphere 6

Krista Hotel Boutique, Bonpland 1665, Palermo Hollywood
Tel: 4771 4697 www.kristahotel.com.ar
Rates: US$90–140

When more than a dozen undercover agents failed to prevent the loss of President Bush's daughter Barbara's handbag during their stay in Buenos Aires, the news broke while they were lodging at the Krista. Like The Cocker hotel in San Telmo, the Krista slickly pulls off that well-designed, homely feel. The 10 rooms all access an indoor or outdoor patio of some

sorts. It's a cheekily designed little maze, perfect for lovers or, indeed, the undercover traveller. Aside from a slightly creepy panelled room, all of the *habitaciones* are the kind your mother would want you to sleep in: clean, stylishly simple and with bedside tables for bedtime reading. Christina, the owner, will not mind, however, if you stumble in late from a night out in Palermo Hollywood, where this hotel is to be found. The wavy haired Christina will have breakfast ready and waiting in the bright sitting room wing of the lobby.

Style 8, Location 8, Atmosphere 8

Mansión Vitraux, Carlos Calvo 369, San Telmo
Tel: 4300 6886   www.mansionvitraux.com
Rates: $170–200

Add a few beats to tango and you have electro-tango. Deck out a 12-bed-room San Telmo building with a couple of swimming pools, a spa, sauna and Jacuzzi, fill its cellar with wine, tack on a chill-out lounge, make the rooms look futuristic and glam, and you have the Mansión Vitraux. The brain child of Rodolfo Hernández, who until not so long ago was supplying shampoo, soap and tooth brushes to the Sheraton, Intercontinental and Holiday Inn hotels. This is the latest addition – opened mid 2007

– to San Telmo's elusive scene, in which previously The Cocker was the only hotel worth mentioning. The Mansión Vitraux continues The Cocker's and 647's (see Drink) lead of bringing modern design to a crumbling part of Buenos Aires and have, to a certain extent, helped reignite the San Telmo revival, which for a moment looked as if it would peter out when 647 struggled to fill. The 12 rooms are deliberately skewed, the lounge is designed for sipping Argentine wine, and the area's only real spa, make the Mansión

Vitraux an equally hip alternative to The Cocker.

Style 8, Location 8, Atmosphere 8

Marriott Plaza Hotel, Florida 1005, Retiro
Tel: 4318 3000   www.marriotplaza.com.ar
Rates: US$250–400

Ernesto Tornquist, who built this hotel back in 1909, must have had a vast workforce to have completed the building's construction in less than a year. What was, and still is, an architectural jewel in Buenos Aires' crown became the Marriott Plaza Hotel in 1994. The Marriott chain is not renowned for its finesse – the upholstery and 1970s pub carpets here score *nul points* for style – but in this case, the attractions of this Parisian-style building, such as its U-shaped façade and Plaza bar, a stalwart in Buenos Aires' drinking scene, justify the Marriott Plaza's inclusion here. And the location is right on the

money for charm. The hotel sits over Plaza San Martin – San Martin is a national hero – beside the Kavanagh building, which at 120 metres high was South America's tallest building when built in 1953. The Plaza is bathed in purple blossom during springtime when the jacaranda trees flower from October to November, so book a room that looks out over it – they have satisfyingly vertigo-enhancing terraces. There is also an outdoor pool and sun deck with views of the Plaza, plus a large modern gym and sauna for toning up before a night out.

Style 5, Location 9, Atmosphere 7

Melia Recoleta Plaza, Posadas 1557, Recoleta
Tel: 5353 4000 www.solmelia.com
Rates: US$230–300

There was no stargazer jacuzzi on top of this former apartment tower when Eva Peron lived here. The building's mural, donated by Juan Domingo Peron, Evita's husband, who was Argentina's president three times between

1946 and his death in 1974, overlooks the lobby. This is the boutique version of the Melia chain, so do not confuse it with the large and rather tacky downtown branch. With only 52 rooms, all recently fitted with the latest mod-cons, you have a comfortable base. Most importantly, though, you have a plucky Recoleta location – where Posadas crosses Callao street – which gives you access to all parts of the city via Libertador Avenue. The Jazz Voyeur restaurant/bar is the resident eatery, but try Sottovocce (Avenida del Liberatador 1098, tel: 4807 6691) around the corner for an Italian spaghetti charge-up.

Style 6, Location 7, Atmosphere 6

My BA Hotel, Zabala 1925, Belgrano
Tel: 4787 5765 www.mybahotel.com
Rates: US$140–220

A 'mini-break from Buenos Aires' relentless pace', My BA Hotel is a brand new 1940s-styled boutique getaway in Belgrano where they aim to treat you as part of the family. A two-day stay here will recharge the batteries and have you ready to fight fire with fire once again in Buenos Aries' party hives, so if you need some time out you know where to come. Located inconspicuously amid las Barrancas de Belgrano ('banks of Belgrano') near the cricket pitch, this is as peaceful an area as you will find in Capital Federal: it has

trees, schools, hospitals and what *porteños* call 'real Argentines'; it is named after Manuel Belgrano, a politician and military leader, who also created the national flag. The hotel has 10 rooms, but spend the extra US$35 and book a deluxe room or fork out US$220 on the charming My Suite, which will send you right back to the days of bowler hats. For River Plate fans, the football team's Monumental stadium, where Argentina won the 1978 Football World Cup, is within walking distance. Puerta Uno is your local bar.

Style 8, Location 7, Atmosphere 7

La Otra Orilla, Julian Alvarez 1779 (between Costa Rica and Soler), Palermo Viejo
Tel: 4867 4070   www.otraorilla.com.ar
Rates: US$35–65

La Otra Orilla ('the other shore') - borders on the hostel category because of its prices, but, nevertheless, is an endearing venue for a little Latin romance. Technically, La Otra Orilla's claim to be a Palermo Viejo hotel is a little bold, since it's located on the southern side of Avenida Scalabrini Ortiz (where most people believe Palermo Viejo ends). However, La Otra Orilla is only a few minutes' walk from the boutique shops and restaurants that the area is so famous for. (Be careful crossing the Avenida on your way there.)

Cecilia Ramos Mejia and her husband Alejandro Braun opened this bed-and-breakfast-style hotel in 2001 during the last crash and have been booked out since the tourists poured in after the 2002 devaluation of the peso. There are seven rooms: four are cosy and slick enough for the choosiest of travellers, but two share a bathroom. There is  one suite overlooking the small, busy garden. Book it. If it's unavailable, choose the Bamboo, Violeta or Lino rooms, which all have puffed double beds and a warmth to them – not that you'll ever be cold in Buenos Aires.

Style 5, Location 7, Atmosphere 7

Palacio Duhau Park Hyatt, Avenida Alvear 1661, Recoleta

Tel: 5171 1234 www.buenosaires.park.hyatt.com
Rates: US$380–4,400

This impressive hotel is one of our top choices in Buenos Aires. Part modern tower, designed to depict the future of Buenos Aires, and part palace, the Palacio Duhau Park Hyatt – which opened in 2006 – is the sexiest building in Recoleta. Formerly owned by the Duhau family, the Palacio Duhau was built in 1934 by French architect Leon Dourge. As the family grew, the palace was divided up until it became a rabbit warren of flats. That's when the Park Hyatt empire snapped up the property. The hotel now seamlessly incorporates vintage glamour with state-of-the-art design. Nowhere else in Buenos Aires will you find sofas made by the Ferrari seat designers beside a room coated in 17th-century French panelling from a Normandy castle. The palace and the tower are linked by an underground tunnel lined with modern art and together serve up 165 rooms. Ask for one of the 23 rooms; 12 of which are suites – in the Palacio Duhau; you want the palace, not the tower. There is no outdoor bathing here, but there is a

25-metre underground pool amid an 8,000 square-metre spa. In the drinking department, the oak bar – with that Normandy panelling – and a subterranean wine and cheese layer await you. Outside, Carlos Thays, who designed Buenos Aires' botanical gardens, has landscaped a 'Paradise Found' garden on what used to be the Duhau family's football pitch. The resident Gioia restaurant is unbeatable for its outdoor lunch buffet.

Style 10, Location 9/10, Atmosphere 8

Palermo 1551, Acuna de Figueroa 1551, Palermo Viejo
Tel: 4867 1310 www.1551palermo.com
Rates: US$50–200

The Luxury Master Penthouse Suite and the poolside Garden Suite make Palermo 1551 sound like an internationally renowned boutique hotel. Think again. This is a slightly underground playboy pad, formerly a family residence, with two souped-up rooms and five others not worth booking. Aside from the Costa Petit hotel and Home, you will not find two finer love dens in

Palermo Viejo. The hotel's layout comprises a two-storey building overlooking the pool and the toolshed-cum-Garden Suite. Service-wise, the attitude is quite *laissez-faire*, but at least cleaning staff keep things tidy. Obnoxious and fun, the Luxury Master, reached via a rustic depot lift, includes a jacuzzi, an out-of-place urinal, its own sun deck and a king-size bed which overlooks the pool garden. The Garden Suite is less pimp palace, more Casanova den, with thin white drapes hanging from all corners of the bed, but with more of a bath than a Jacuzzi. The garden needs some work, and the huge sitting room is a mishmash of styles, but this is a great 'how's-your-father' hideaway pad: slightly messy, with an element of boisterous finesse.

Style 8, Atmosphere 8, Location 8

Panamericano, Carlos Pellegrini 551, Centre
Tel: 4348 5000 www.panamericanobuenosaires.com
Rates: US$260–400

Sight-seeing could not be easier at the Panamericano. If you close one eye when facing Avenida 9 de Julio – said to be the widest avenue in the world – from the hotel, you will still see either the obelisk or the opera house. The Obelisco, which marks the centre of the city, and the Teatro Colón, with its famed acoustics, perch right in front of the Panamericano's two 23-floor towers. With 363 rooms, it's surprising how few guests soak up the view from the North Tower's rooftop pool aquarium, a vantage point from which

almost every postcard photo you see of Buenos Aires' obelisk will have been taken. The rooms are in the classic Ritz Carlton style of oak furniture and all have soundproofed glass to keep the roar of taxi horns *afuera*. No matter how soft the complimentary bath robes may be in the rooms that face the river, it's not worth staying here unless your window looks onto Avenida 9 de Julio. Resident restaurant Tomo Uno is also a must on your travel itinerary, while tango hotspot Café Tortoni (see Party) are a few minutes' walk away, as is mega club Palacio Alsina (see Party).

Style 6, Location 10, Atmosphere 6

Sofitel Buenos Aires, Arroyo 841, Retiro
Tel: 4131 0000 www.sofitelbuenosaires.com.ar
Rates: US$250–550

The Sofitel is tucked away down Arroyo street in the neoclassical Bencich Tower adjacent to Plaza San Martin, a block away from the site of the 1992 Israeli Embassy bombing. Built in 1929 for Yugoslav ship owner Mihanvich, who wanted immigrants to see the 80-metre skyscraper as they arrived at the port, and developed in 2000 by architects Daniel Fernandez & Asociados and Pierre-Yves Rochon, who designed the New York Sofitel, this 20-floor pile has been cleverly linked to two matching buildings in front of the tower by a glass roof. The transparent ceiling unites the three buildings to form a beautifully lit vitreous lobby, which guests must walk through to reach the foot of the tower where the front desk is located. Visually, this is a master-

piece, so make sure the bell-boy takes your bags before you enter the hotel so that you can look skyward. Up in the tower, the magnolia rooms do not quite do the lobby justice, but the marble bathrooms, seductive mustard upholstery and soft lighting will ensure you sleep well.

Below the tower is a fitness centre and a narrow lap pool. Back up again to the lobby, the nicely understated Arroyo café is filled with mix of businessmen and stylish Europeans sipping coffee to the sound of chilled eclectic beats.

Style 9, Location 7, Atmosphere 8

Youkali Hotel, Estados Unidos 1393, San Telmo

Tel: 4381 6064   www.youkali.com.ar
Rates: US$45–85

'It's just so Buenos Aires,' says the endearingly camp German owner Gerd Tepass as he leans over the counter dressed in a wife-beater. The good news, or bad news, depending on your point of view, is that this is one of the most popular hotels in Buenos Aires for porn and glamour magazine shoots. *Playboy* calls it the most exotic and erotic hotel in the city. Gerd will proudly flip through the magazines – including a Taiwanese title – with

guests during check-in and will probably tell you he is currently considering offers from television companies to shoot hardcore porn here. So far he has resisted a $3,000 daily fee for renting out a room as a Harry Horndog set. So there is still at least an air of cleanliness about the place. Formerly the Boquita Pintadas hotel, inspired by Manuel Puig's novel, the Youkali is named after Jewish German composer Kurt Weill's tango song 'Youkali', about a land of longing that doesn't exist. And the hotel itself if appropriately inconspicuous in Constitución, on the borders of tango central San Telmo. Of the five rooms, the Ruwenzori room, whose bed is decorated with carvings of the heads of Egyptian princesses, is most popular. All rooms are spacious, with rustic en-suite bathrooms in turn-of-the-century style, and come equipped with DVD players and, crucially, air conditioning. But as Gerd puts it: 'It's the real Buenos Aires life. Actors, film producers and musicians love it here.' The plumbing, however, is currently being reviewed.

Style 7/8, Location 5, Atmosphere 8

OUTSIDE BUENOS AIRES

El Calafate

Esplendor El Calafate, Pte. Peron 1143, El Calafate, Santa Cruz
Tel: 5217 5700 www.esplendorcalafate.com
Rates: US$170–200

If you have visited the Iguazu Falls, then you must see the glaciers (see Play). Both feature on the list of natural wonders of the world, but if pressed, we would take the glaciers over the falls. The world's only advancing glacier, the

Perito Moreno, will make your jaw drop for an embarrassingly long time. Truly unforgettable. The glaciers are a 45-minute drive away from El Calafate, where most hotels are located. El Calafate's first design hotel, the Esplendor, was unveiled in late 2006 and follows on from its stylish sister back in Buenos Aires. With views over Lago Argentino, this is the most striking position in what is an otherwise barren landscape. The project was designed by Mauro Bernardini and Cecilia

Timossi, who have provided 57 maroon-and-chocolate coloured rooms in the Esplendor's slick minimalist style, but have chucked a bed rug into the equation, given the chilly surroundings. The sitting room is a playful mess of furniture with stunning views of the lake. Splendid.

Style 8/9, Location 9, Atmosphere 9

Iguazu

Sheraton Internacional Iguazu Resort, Parque Nacional Iguazú, Iguazú
Tel: (3757) 491800   www.sheraton.com
Rates: US$250–500

Jeremy Irons successfully scales the Iguazu falls in his habit during the blockbuster-hit *The Mission*. The view from the Sheraton is rather better than the one Jeremy – or his stunt man – enjoyed. Without a trip to the Iguazu falls, your trip to the Argentine is not complete. While you can take a day trip up to the falls – 18 metres higher than Niagara and wider than the Victoria falls (see Play) – dusk and dawn views of the 275 falls crashing down 82 metres are stunning, and the sound made in the jungle by around 400 species of bird (not to mention the odd killer cat) is deafening. The Sheraton is the only

Argentine hotel with direct views of the falls, so do not be tempted to book in at any other, despite their claims to be a few minutes from the action. Built for tourists during the 1978 World Cup – when Argentina beat the Dutch in

the final – this looks like a structure erected in a hurry. It's a concrete slab of 180 rooms, half of which face the hotspot. With the looks of a Costa del Sol/Cancun resort, all eyes are fixed on the clouds of spray sent up by the millions of tons of water crashing into the river below. The Sheraton has a particularly warm swimming pool, but walk down to the falls, swim in the river beside them and, literally, be nibbled at by curious fish. Try not to ignore the Park's rules and walk down to the falls alone during the evening. If the noise of the falls doesn't get to you, a puma, jaguar or snake possibly will. The restaurant serves excellent pacu fish.

Style 7, Location 10, Atmosphere 7

Mendoza

Cavas Wine Lodge, Costaflores s/n, Alto Agrelo, Mendoza
Tel: +54 (0) 261 410 6927/28 (International) / +54 (0)261 15 454 4118
Rates: US$240–350

You are in the middle of a 35-acre vineyard with panoramic views of the Andes. You have finished a day of wine tasting – remembering to spit, of course – in Mendoza's vineyards and you have just paid a visit to the Cavas' spa. The massage has put you in the zone: hop into your plunge pool, sip on a glass of Malbec – have a gulp if you like, there is plenty more. The clouds are poking over the snow-capped peaks. The air temperature drops, but the water is still nice and warm. Your frisky, futuristic, 70-square-metre adobe bungalow hut – called a 'vignette' – is one of 14 on the property. After an al

fresco shower, it's time to head up to the dramatic white Spanish colonial-style house, where chef Sebastian Flores is cooking the beef to go with your bottle of Malbec-Cabernet Sauvignon blend. This is the only way to sample Mendoza's wine region. Hotel marketer Cecilia Diaz Chuit and her husband, vineyard expert Martin Rigal, have combined forces to create Cavas Wine Lodge, which opened in 2005. Now, with increasing exposure, they are not short of guests. Book one of the five vignettes furthest from the main house (well in advance) for the best views. The Park Hyatt opened its new Mendoza branch in 2006, but Cavas Wine Lodge is the more authentic, if slightly eccentric, choice. Rates vary from US$240 in the low season (3 May to 14 Sept) to US$350 in the high season (1 Jan to 2 May).

Style 8, Location 10, Atmosphere 8

Punta del Este

Posada del Faro, Calle de La Bahia (corner of Timonel), Faro Jose Ignacio, Uruguay
Tel: +598 486 2110 www.posadadelfaro.com
Rates: US$90–550

The tiny Jose Ignacio is a hamlet-like group of houses that bobble up on a point marked by a lighthouse. This is the highly understated, cool little

brother of Punta del Este. It's the destination of clued-up socialites, who head down to the beach in their pick-ups at around 3pm after waking up from the night before. When in Punta, you need a car anyway, so do not be disturbed by the distance (40km) and take it as a hint that finger-on-the-pulse Argentines – and the odd Uruguayan – drive here from Punta every afternoon. Posada del Faro is a 12-room beach house hotel decked out with hammocks and bamboo sun shelters, and decorated with whitewashed walls, blue doors and the odd bikini-clad bombshell adorning the stunning pool. All this just 30m from the beach. Opened in 1991 by residents Jose and Carla Garcia, Posada del Faro, which roughly translates as 'little house by the lighthouse', is everything the Mantra hotel (listed below) is not. This is a relaxed paradise from which you can assault Punta's party scene (which runs from the end of December to mid-February) from a distance. The surfing here is also arguably the best in the area.

Style 10, Location 9, Atmosphere 7

Mantra Resort, Spa and Casino, Route 10, Stop 48, La Barra, Punta del Este, Uruguay

Tel: +598 (42) 771 000 www.mantraresort.com
Rates: US$300

Innocently dipped all in white on a hilltop in the trees, Mantra is anything but: '*Mantra es lo más top*' (which translates as something like 'this hotel is the coolest, hippest choice'). Of course, Argentines seem to decide what goes and what doesn't in this part of Uruguay. Mantra is the opposite of the

Posada del Faro hotel being just minutes from the relentless action of 'La Barra', the pivotal area of Punta del Este's scene – a scene that has exploded over the past four years. Parties used to be hosted by influential

personalities, but now glossy magazines and model agencies dominate the guest lists. Your reference to Mantra should help matters. Dramatically cascading down the hillside, Mantra's dens and lobby all overlook the pool area and casino and all peer over the Atlantic Ocean. Like the exterior, the 88 rooms and 12 suites have all been given the puritan bleached treatment, so don't forget the sunglasses – not that you would in a place like this. The 'boutique casino' – sunglasses optional – sets the tone here, as does the pool, where Argentina's finest show off the latest in plastic surgery and their brilliant ability to make you feel like a pervert for looking at them. The hotel is not as pristine as it was in 2004 when it opened – the odd blade of grass may stick out here and there – but Mantra, for now, remains the top dog in Punta.

Style 8, Location 9, Atmosphere 10

Salta

House of Jasmines, Ruta Nacional Numero 51, Kilómetro 11, La Merced Chica, Salta, Argentina
Tel: 0387 4972 002/2005   www.houseofjasmines.com
Rates: US$375–475

Salta is tucked away in the Lerma Valley, 1,187 metres above sea level at the foot of the 20 de Febrero and San Bernardo mountains. Here, the sandy rock formations are famous for their beautiful cocktail of green, orange and silver tones, while the city is steeped in its past – its Diaguita-Calchaqui and

Inca roots and its 16th-century Spanish colonial architecture. Just outside the city, House of Jasmines can be found up a tree-lined driveway that leads to a farmhouse owned by actor Robert Duvall and his wife, Luciana. Once a century-old ruin, this is now a boutique farmhouse hotel – opened in 2004 – with seven rooms. All have sturdy wrought-iron four-poster beds, all are filled with antique goodies and all are perfumed by the surrounding gardens. Pick one of the two suites that have panoramic views and lead out onto the garden. There is a nicely sized pool to go with the 300-acre farm. The Salta province is bordered by Chile, Bolivia and Paraguay, as well as six Argentine provinces.

Style 9, Location 9, Atmosphere 6

San Carlos de Bariloche

Llao Llao Hotel & Resort, Av. Bustillo, Km 25 outside Bariloche
Tel: 02944 448530 www.llaollao.com
Rates: US$175–1,770

There are plenty of hotels in and outside Bariloche, but the Llao Llao is unquestionably the biggest hitter of them all, demanding international fame for its breathtaking position and the view from its golf course. The hotel sits below Mount Lopez on a hill between Lake Nahuel Huapi and Lake Moreno, which looks tantalizingly bluer and bluer the higher you climb. If ever there was a blade of grass to build on, then this is it. After burning down in 1938,

being rebuilt in 1940 by Alejandro Bustillo and then refurbished in 1993, the building looks like a scaled-up version of a ski chalet. Inside the hotel has gone for the classic look: cypress and pine-log walls, stone fireplace, antler chandeliers. On the downside, with 42 new rooms, the Llao Llao is becoming a little impersonal and, because of its fame, there are a few too many tourists in the car park for our liking. You will, however, be too amazed by the scenery to care. Bariloche's ski centre, the Cerro Catedral – where the two separate sides of the mountain have now been linked to each other – is 17 miles away, so the Llao Llao have built another branch up there. For polo in the area, consider the Arelauquen Golf and Country Club (www.are-lauquen.com).

Style 9, Location 10, Atmosphere 7

San Isidro (15–20 mins from BA)

Hotel del Casco, Av. del Libertador 16170, San Isidro
Tel: 4732 3993   www.hoteldelcasco.com.ar
Rates: US$135–200

San Isidro is the northern suburb of Buenos Aires where Argentina's high and mighty families continue to breed – usually no fewer than five children per piece – and enjoy the sunshine from beside their pools. Despite an incessant snobbery, probably only matched by the English – many families here, particularly in La Horqueta, insist they are of the finest Irish or English bloodlines – you will enjoy staying in San Isidro. Hotel del Casco is dwarfed by San Isidro's cathedral, but with 12 rooms – 8 currently being added, along with a new pool – you come here for the 1890s guesthouse experience, away from Buenos Aires' smog. Originally owned by the Maiol family, Hotel del Casco has that long-lost 'Spanish *don*' feel to it, with high ceilings, pillars, sculptures, a garden and a peaceful internal patio perfect for an early evening drink. This is not a hotel for the nocturnal warrior. You come here for a break from Buenos Aires and access to Argentina's outdoor pursuits. It's a 20-minute drive from the centre of Buenos Aires and is surrounded by golf courses and the San Isidro Jockey Club – where races such as the Carlos Pelegrini are run in December, and where the Jockey Club Polo Open is played at the end of September – and it also has direct access to some of the River Plate's largest yacht clubs. Polo players are 20 minutes

from Pilar, Argentina's high-goal polo centre. The railway station is a block away, although a taxi will cost around US$40 to the centre of town – where we all know things can go one of two ways.

Style 8, Location 6, Atmosphere 7

La Pascuala Delta Lodge, Aroyo des Canas, Delta del Rio Panara, Buenos Aires
Tel: 4728 1395/1253 (lodge); 4378 0982 (reservation) www.lapascuala.com
Rates: US$147–176

When you're floating down the Las Cañas stream on the Delta del Paraná, it feels like it could be the Amazon. Pass me a beer from our paddleboat's

built-in cooler, please. La Pascuala Delta Lodge proves that the Tigre's delta region is no longer just a day-trip destination for wakeboarders. It's now possible to unwind from the city, in total luxury, submerged in a green wilderness surrounded by water. Just half an hour's drive from the centre of Buenos Aires, La Pascuala's 15 air-conditioned and mosquito-netted bungalow huts are suspended over the water, nestled among the trees. All the bungalows are connected to the main building through wooden walkways, which lead to a riverside infinity pool, spa, restaurant and, perhaps most enticingly, an open bar. Back down the walkways after a wakeboarding session, fishing trip or another boozy paddleboat drift, have a read under your bathtub's rigged reading light. For the not-so-rugged jungle lover who loves a little bit of pampering, this is paradise.

Style 9, Location 9, Atmosphere 7

eat...

Sharpen your steak knives and stay clear of the aeroplane food before touching down at Ezeiza airport. You'll need as much of an appetite as possible if you are to dent Argentina's beef mountain. Incredibly large, tender, juicy steaks await you, as well as delicious offal, sweetbreads and intestines. Argentines hate to waste any part of the animal, so if you're a little squeamish check what you're ordering with your waiter. *Bife de chorizo* (rib-eye steak) or *bife de lomo* (sirloin steak) and *bife de costilla* (T-bone steak) are the staple cuts, while *tiro de asado* and *matambre* (a thin flank cut unique to Argentina) require more work but are seen as tastier by some, and finally *vacio* (flank) is a typical *gaucho* cut. Argentines, particularly the squeamish, like their beef *cocido* (well done), so knowing the words for medium rare (*al punto*)and rare (*jugoso*) is just as important to know as the words for beer (*cerveza*) and God (Diego Maradona) in this town. La Cabrera (in Palermo Viejo) and La Brigada (in San Telmo) are our favourites for unadulterated beef-bashing, although it is a constant on all menus.

Modern Argentine cuisine is developing swiftly as a new breed of chefs reinterpret traditional dishes. Desde el Alma in Palermo Viejo (intimate) and Sucre (fashionable) will give you an indication of the direction in which Argentine cuisine is headed.

Away from the slaughterhouses, Buenos Aires is cottoning on to the demand for an alternative to beef. The immediate and fashionable substitute is sushi. Health-conscious Argentines unsurprisingly love low-calorie and low-carb sushi, and hundreds of restaurants have sprung up in affluent areas. The standard of sushi in Buenos Aires is varied, so choose carefully. Osaka is the trendiest of the sushi bars, while Dashi (Fitz Roy 1613, tel: 4776 3600, www.dashi.com.ar) also produces high-quality sushi in a hip setting. Little Rose provides the most seductive environment, while the hip Dominga also includes sushi on its mega menu. Alternatively, choose an authentic Japanese restaurant near Chinatown where the sushi is far superior. Nihonbashi tops the bill and attracts a mostly Japanese audience, as well as clued-up *porteños* out to impress their dates with new-found chopstick abilities.

European culture is still influential in Argentina, which means high-quality French and Italian food is always available. Most restaurants will field pasta as a substitute for stomach-heavy beef. As far as specialist Italians go, Piegari is our favourite, while Lucky Luciano and Guido's are also excellent.

Many restaurants in Buenos Aires look spectacular, but disappoint gastronomically. The city's restaurant/bar culture is to blame, and you'll find that in a few notable restaurants the standard of the food will not match the atmosphere. Casa Cruz, El Gran Bar Danzon, Rubia y Negra and 647 (see Drink) are all restaurant/bars we think it's best just to head for a drink.

In terms of districts, Palermo Viejo and Palermo Hollywood have exploded onto Buenos Aires' culinary scene and are the most fashionable places to eat. Outside these areas, in Recoleta and the centre of town, the kitchens tend to be a little more serious. Oviedo, Tomo Uno and Resto are arguably the finest in the city.

Do remember that while Las Cañitas and Puerto Madero are packed with restaurants, few Argentines with an ounce of fashion sense would consider eating there. These two areas are earmarked for tourists and should be avoided, although we have included Arguibel (Las Cañitas) and Puerto Madero's most famous restaurant, Cabaña Las Lilas (see Snack).

In addition to our selections, you could try one of Dan Perlman's private dinner parties (look at www.casasaltshaker.com to be selected for a place at one of the parties) held once or twice a week.

Top 10 restaurants in Buenos Aires:
1. Oviedo
2. La Cabrera
3. Osaka
4. Tomo Uno
5. Desde el Alma
6. Thymus
7. Resto
8. Sudestada
9. La Brigada
10. Lucky Luciano

Top 5 restaurants for food:
1. Oviedo
2. Tomo Uno
3. La Cabrera
4. Thymus
5. Resto

Top 5 restaurants for service:
1. Agraz
2. Nihonbashi
3. Resto
4. Oviedo
5. Guido's

Top 5 restaurants for atmosphere:
1. Osaka
2. Olsen
3. Green Bamboo
4. Sudestada
5. Dominga

Agraz (Caesar Park Hotel), Posadas 1232, Recoleta
Tel: 4819 1129
Open: daily, noon–3.30pm and 8pm–midnight. AR$85

After an early evening's shopping at Patio Bullrich, walk across Posadas Street and into the Caesar Park Hotel, hand your bags to a bellhop and roll into dinner at Agraz. Looking like every five-star hotel's archetypal lobby restaurant, the feel is one of dining on a cruise liner. Fears are quietly dispelled as warm bread and hummus are brought with Rodrigo Tosso's menu.

Like Tomo Uno and Resto, everything is about the food and not the surroundings, which tend to include the serious suits on expenses that stay at the Caesar. Inventive pasta and delicate fish dishes are omnipresent on an ever-changing menu here, and the waitresses, rigorously trained by Rodrigo, are well versed in all things *vino*. Apart from the slightly sterile atmosphere Agraz is a delight and if you are seriously impressed by the food you can attend one of Rodrigo's cookery classes (see Play). Turn up laden with shopping for an early dinner before hitting the bars in your new outfit.

Food 8/9, Service 10, Atmosphere 5

Arguibel, Andrés Arguibel 2826, Las Cañitas
Tel: 4899 0070
Open: 7.30pm–1am. Closed Sundays. AR$70

This is a beer-slugging part of town, known for the strip of bars down Báez street. Head to Arguibel for a proper dinner before rolling on for a drink at

Soul Café or to Kandi (see Drink), where the food is awful but the crowd beautiful. After La Corte restaurant closed in Las Cañitas, this area's culinary scene was never going to grow as fast as it could have done. Arguibel seems a little out of place, therefore. The building is a slickly converted warehouse

with an art gallery overlooking the ground floor from urban metallic stages. Specialities include pork ribs wrapped in bacon with garlic potato, as well as the classic fillet steak. If Arguibel is empty, you are just around the corner from the ever-packed Campo Bravo, whose meat is supplied from the owner's abattoir, and opposite Novecento, which has New York, Punta del Este and Miami branches. Arguibel is the quieter choice of the three, but is Las Cañitas' most stylish restaurant by some distance. In front of Arguibel is Penal Uno, a bar owned by legendary polo players Adolfo Cambiasso, two Heguy brothers and Bartolome Castagnola, all of whom have won the Argentine Open on several occasions. Penal Uno is often closed, but if you're lucky, is open during November and December during the Open. The 'cathedral of polo' – the Campo Argentino de Polo – is two blocks away.

Food 8, Service 8, Atmosphere 7

Bar Uriarte, Uriarte 1572, Palermo Viejo
Tel: 4834 6004 www.baruriarte.com.ar
Open: daily, noon–2.30am   AR$80

You will see the chefs flashing their pans as you stroll into Uriarte – 'stroll' being the operative word at this stylish eatery. Rumour has it that a waitress was fired for smiling too much at the customers, so keep your game face

on. Bar Uriarte is of the same ilk as El Gran Bar Danzon (from the stable of restaurateurs who also co-own Sucre, see Drink), but it has its nose in front as a dining location because the music is pumped out at a more civilized volume and there is more room for cuddling in cavernous sofas, as well as al fresco dining. The stuffed mushroom starter has garnered quite a reputation in this part of Palermo Viejo, and the main courses, while Argentine-based, have a touch of the Mediterranean and Italian to them. On your way back from the bathroom, peer down and watch the chefs scuttling around the urban metal kitchen creating delicious morsels. We recommend you stay for a drink after dinner, but consider Casa Cruz (see Drink), one of Argentina's most fashionable restaurants, for further cocktails. Controversially we must say steer clear of Casa Cruz's kitchen, but it is certainly worth popping down the road to try one of their celebrated bartender Ines' cocktails.

Food 8, Service 8, Atmosphere 8

Bereber, Armenia 1880, Palermo Viejo

Tel: 4833 5662

Open: daily, 8.30pm–1am   AR$60

Plonk yourself down on a Moroccan cushion and direct your thoughts to happy contemplation: how much spicy marinade you are going to lace your lamb Habra and couscous with? The owners of Asian favourite Green Bamboo bring you Bereber, a mouthful to pronounce at first, but a name you'll get used to hearing in the alternative-to-beef-restaurant conversations. The first floor boasts an open-air terrace, but the ground-floor 'Let's lie down and eat Marrakech style' option is advised for those looking to get fully into the King Mohammed VI role. Stick to *caiprinhas* as warm-up cocktails, as the barman loves holidaying in Brazil, and he is always too busy, usually mending his till, to shake anything more complicated. Located right beside Plaza Palermo Viejo, Bereber is your Moroccan launch-pad for an evening out at Mundo Bizarro, Congo or 878, followed by Podesta or Club Niceto.

Food 7/8, Service 6, Atmosphere 8/9

La Bourgogne (Alvear Palace Hotel), Ayacucho 2027, Recoleta
Open: noon–3pm, 8.30pm–late Mon–Sat. Closed Sundays.   AR$100

There are times when the table manners your mother taught you don't quite measure up to the challenges that life throws your way. So it is when you are confronted with mozzarella and olives to be eaten out of champagne glasses problems can arise. The fish, rabbit, venison and lamb main courses, however, are a little more run of the mill in the table etiquette department, as is your table-bound champagne glass, which you will never

see the bottom of. Jean Paul Bondoux has acquired quite a reputation in this part of South America, opening restaurants in Punta del Este and Mendoza to accompany his Alvear Palace Hotel headquarters. He's the kind of Frenchman that dresses in chinos, Ralph Lauren shirts, suede loafers and kisses you on the cheek every time he laughs – a charming man and an inventive chef. Head downstairs to La Bourgogne's basement instead of the main restaurant, where jazz bands perform live on Friday evenings. It's a bit of a conversation basher, as the sax player (eyes tight shut, of course) and drummer (likewise) fill this former wine cellar with their hypnotic sounds. La Bourgogne's basement is an upmarket and original environment for a date you need to impress. Jean Paul's cookbooks are on sale upstairs. Once you've impressed, Cartier, in front of the Alvear, will sell you the ring.

Food 8, Atmosphere 7, Service 9

Brasserie Petanque, Defensa 596, San Telmo
Tel: 4342 7930   www.brasseriepetanque.com
Open: 12.30–3pm Mon; 8pm–1.30am Tues–Sat; 12.30pm–1am Sun   AR$50

We would be grateful if you would not confuse us with a bistro, say Brasserie Petanque. For unlike brasseries – apparently – bistros are not large, noisy, casual or affordable; nor do they have good country wines, a simple traditional menu, or plenty of beers from all around the world. That's all very well, but proprietor Pascal Meyer's mission statement is a little off. In fact, this quaintly lit French bistro-cum-brasserie is far more stylish than he makes it out to be, which is precisely the reason why this San Telmo establishment regularly brims with Buenos Aires' foodies. A five-minute walk

from San Telmo's Plaza Dorrego, Pentanque sits on the corner of two typically tired-looking streets. The interior, however, apart from the waiters, is
tout French, as is *le menu*, which includes *canard*, *lapin* and, of course, *steak
frîtes* for the Argentine beef addict. Afterwards, try 647 for a late drink on a
Friday evening, remembering to dress to dazzle the bouncers. If not, ask for
Alfonso and tell him we sent you.

Food 8, Service 8, Atmosphere 8

La Brigada, Estados Unidos 465, San Telmo

Tel: 4361 5557

Open: noon–3pm, 8pm–midnight. Closed Mondays. AR$80

La Brigada recently won a poll for the best *parilla* (grill restaurant) in the
city, which is quite an accolade. We say La Brigada is San Telmo's finest,
closely followed by El Desnivel (see Snack). They call chef-owner Hugo
Echevarrieta the '*Maestro Parillero*' (grill master). He's a little rough around
the edges and his staff are terrified of him, partly because he looks like a
football hooligan, but mainly because at times he acts like one. But it's okay.
The man is indeed a master craftsman and the service is better for his
bluntness. Away from the kitchen knives, the décor of this duplex meat
house incorporates *gaucho* memorabilia, in keeping with the traditions of

the *parilla*, but most of the walls and entire ceilings are covered in soccer
scarves and shirts. This is as bona fide an Argentine restaurant as you'll find:
juicy steak cooked with the fat on to add flavour, tender short-rib roasts,

sirloin and fillet steaks and renowned goat sweetbreads and cow intestines are all on the menu – with *milongas* (songs and dances) playing in the background and, of course, football. We think Mr Echevarrieta is a Boca fan, but dared not ask. If in doubt, remind him that Jorge Burruchaga scored the winner for Argentina in the 1986 World Cup win over Germany.

Food 9, Service 8, Atmosphere 8

La Cabrera, Cabrera 5099, Palermo Viejo
Tel: 4831 7002
Open: 12.30–4pm, 8pm–1am. Closed Monday lunch.   AR$80

La Cabrera has to be the top *parilla* in the city. The advantage La Cabrera has over La Brigada is that it sits right in the heart of Palermo Viejo's nocturnal explosion, it has a little more social oomph than La Brigada, and the atmosphere around the grill is a little less life-threatening. Guests are administered champagne while they wait for a table – and you'll have to

wait, so do not be late for your booking. The interior is a cosy but simple mesh of white walls splashed with modern art, while the pressed white table linen weighed down  with wine bottles sends out the message that you probably won't leave standing. The simple Argentine food is prepared on Gastón Rivera's surprisingly small grill. Tuck into *provoleta* cheese, *chorizo* and *morcilla* (blood sausage), accompanied by dozens of tasty sauces to start, followed by rib-eye, fillet and beef off-the-bone cuts – a meat feast to be washed down with a full-bodied Malbec. It's all about the quality of the cuts, the pine wood he uses to add flavour, and, of course, timing.

Food 9, Service 9, Atmosphere 9

Centro Vasco Francés, Moreno 1370, Centro
Tel: 4381 5415 www.rvascofrances.com.ar
Open: daily, noon–3.30pm, 8,30pm–midnight   AR$60

Founded in 1895, and now run by Marla Lazarte, this is the Basque capital of
Buenos Aires, with, we are told, more of a French tinge to it than an *Hola
Señor*. Set in the gaping first-floor dining hall of the Basque Cultural Centre,
Centro Vasco Francés is *siempre, pero siempre* packed with around 150 din-
ers, who enjoy the fish and seafood starters before moving on to more
adventurous main courses, such as the dried frogs' legs soaked in garlic. The

menu is, as Basque cuisine is, 'based around the sea and the mountains',
which really means everything is on offer, prepared in a visceral, rustic
manner. Either way, the food is flavoursome and hearty, and scoffed down in
what amounts to a stylized bingo hall. Argentines would be impressed if you
took them here to dinner, so book in advance, and try not to fall down the
steps after dinner like we did.

Food 8/9, Service 7, Atmosphere 7/8

Desde el Alma, Honduras esq. Godoy Cruz, Palermo Viejo
Tel: 4831 5812
Open: 8.30pm–1am. Closed Sundays.   AR$80

Opened in 2002 by Alberto Verdi, Desde el Alma ('from the soul') is said to
be a dangerous place for a man to take a date. He's advised to make sure
he's accompanied by two young ladies, as one will fall in love with chef Lucio
Cantini and the other will fall in love with him for taking her there.

Meanwhile in the heat of his kitchen, simplicity is crucial to Lucio's menu. He produces divine salmon and beef dishes, which are a cut above. Although by now you're probably feeling sick at the sight of the word 'beef', at Desde el Alma they really do deliver, so order the steak fillet with mashed potatoes and a bottle of Malbec. If you really have to deviate, the Patagonian lamb is

superb. Book ahead to reserve the table in front of the fireplace surrounded by snug sofas and illuminated by scented candles, although you will then be the centre of attention. The food, mood and setting are all in the fabulously seductive category and hidden behind wooden shutters, which are only opened 'when things get too hot inside'. Congo (see Drink) is just a few yards down the road for a cooling-off cocktail.

Food 9, Service 8, Atmosphere 8

Dominga, Honduras 5618, Palermo Hollywood
Tel: 4771 4443   AR$75
Open: 12.30–3.30pm, 8.30pm–1am. Closed Saturday lunch and Sundays.

Take a Rastafarian manager, a half-Japanese, half-Argentine menu, a feng shui-ed patio and a snazzy dining room flanked by yellow lighting; add in elegantly arrogant waitresses who strut the floors in heels, and you've encapsulated Dominga in a nutshell. A bizarrely eclectic mix of pompous businessmen and top Argentine male models enjoy dining here with their polo-playing buddies. Surprisingly, given the overly large menu, the quality and freshness of the food is excellent. And the cocktails are faultless – sake-based concoctions have had a renaissance in Buenos Aires recently – making Dominga

one of the top Palermo Hollywood restaurants for style and food, a pair that usually have little association in this town. The spicy *ceviche* soup will moisten the brow, which can then be cooled by fresh sushi, or you could steam right on to the Argentine lamb and risotto classics. Follow your meal with a drink in Las Cañitas' Soul Café or Kandi, not far from the restaurant.

Food 8, Service 8, Atmosphere 9

Green Bamboo, Costa Rica 5802, Palermo Hollywood
Tel: 4775 7050 www.green-bamboo.com.ar
Open: daily, 8.30pm–2.30am   AR$80

Arguably superior to Sudestada, attracting fewer *gatos* than Osaka and with the scariest bearded waiters in the city, Green Bamboo has won plaudits in Palermo Hollywood, an area famous for its gastronomy. Attitude exudes from every porthole of this dark corner of South East Asian cuisine, so try

not to speak too loudly in English, and dress to kill if the terrifyingly tough waiters are to accept you. The bar is cluttered with Asian dragon figures, the 20-odd capacity dining room has that red light zone tinge and the walls are decorated with Asian art. Diners order well-made *mojitos* and enjoy a similar culinary experience to Sudestada, whose starters are superior, and spicy duck inferior, as well as Osaka, whose main courses are similar but include sushi. El Carnal is the closest bar for a post-prandial cocktail (see Drink).

Food 8, Service 7/8, Atmosphere 9

Guido's, República de la India 2843, Palermo
Tel: 4802 2391
Open: noon–4pm, 8pm onwards. Closed Saturdays and Sundays.   AR$80

The ethos here is 'sit down and eat what you are given'. Guido Sosto is famous in this posh Palermo neighbourhood (next to the zoo) for stuffing his customers – who are not allowed to leave the table until they are at the

point of explosion. There is no menu, so tell the waiter what you don't eat and he'll pack your table full of dishes containing everything else. When they are finished, he'll bring more. When they've all gone, it's time for the pasta, and there's lots of that too. If you behave yourself, Guido might let you off pudding, but you have to be on the floor for that to happen. Guido charges 80 pesos a head, unless, seriously, you want to do the washing up. Every inch of the walls are covered in Maradona, Frank Sinatra and Marilyn Monroe pictures, with the odd plastic breast to boot, making it a more relaxed than stylish café. When you leave you'll probably need to call Radio Taxi Premium

(5238 0000), as you won't be walking anywhere after this. If Guido's is full, try Guido's son's place, Lucky Luciano, which is just around the corner on Cerviño.

Food 7, Service 9, Atmosphere 8

Juana M, Carlos Pellegrini 1535, Retiro
Tel: 4326 0462
Open: daily, noon–4pm, 8pm–12.30am   AR$40

Mathematical genius Juana Martyn and her engineer husband Quique were almost down-and-out during the 2000 crash. They gradually cleared out what was at that time the abandoned basement of an orphanage, exterminated the rats and bought in a few tables from Tigre. Juana cooked up her *steak à la moutarde*, and *porteños* gradually came in their hordes – many

paying in IOUs, such was the shortage of cash during the *corralito* (a time when Argentines were only permitted to take out $1,000 per person per month while their money lost around 70% of its value in the bank). Juana M is a long, urban, subterranean vault of a restaurant clad in modern art, where young, fashionable Argentines come for dinner. It's not expensive and the Argentine dishes – the kind your wife cooks for you if you've managed to behave yourself – are tasty and satisfying. Avoid the peppered steak, since the peppercorns are prone to stick to your teeth. But do perch on a high stool over Juana's solid wooden tables, study the meat and pasta dishes on the menu and ask if Sofia Maria Van Thienen, the *New York Times'* favourite Argentine waitress, can attend your table. There is a free, unlimited salad bar and the *caipirinhas* are explosive.

Food 6, Service 7, Atmosphere 8

Little Rose, Armenia 1672, Palermo Viejo
Tel: 4833 9496
Open: 1–4pm, 8.30pm–1am Mon–Sat. Closed Sundays.   AR$60

The décor of this highly sophisticated restaurant is exceptional, the sushi is slightly above average and the location is as perfect as you will find in Palermo Viejo. The Argentine sushi chefs, dressed like Japanese submarine mechanics, are slightly over-the-top, however, especially given that the tuna rolls are inexplicably made with tinned tuna (although in Buenos Aires it is difficult to find the fresh stuff), but the salmon sushi and *sashimi* more than makes up for it. One of Argentina's iconic photographers and one of Little

Rose's owners, Gabriel Roca, took the child portraits hanging on the black walls. And Little Rose happens to be the young lady seen photographed here – the idea being she and her siblings will dine eat here regularly as they get older with new portraits marking the transition of time. The black panelled walls and seductive lighting mean Rose will probably not take full advantage of the restaurant – particularly the sofa booth – until she has the boys knocking on her door. But until then, this seductive first-floor masterpiece has room for anyone with pocket money. The other shareholders of Little Rose are the owners of Mott (see Drink), which is only 30 metres away and great for pre-dinner drinks.

Food 7, Service 9, Atmosphere 9

Lucky Luciano, Cerviño 3943, Palermo

Tel: 4802 1262

Open: daily, 8pm–1am   AR$60

Think stylishly cluttered walls, Buenos Aires' in-crowd of wine buffs, cock-tail-making celebrities and a cellar full of full-blooded Argentine reds. Owned by the Sosto brothers – sons of Guido Sosto who owns the now

iconic Guido's (see page 79) around the corner – but run by Luciano, Argentina's friendliest sommelier this red-painted building is all heart, and you will love it. Chef Silvia Krestchnel, one of the few female head chefs in Buenos Aires and a protégé of Argentine celebri-ty chef Francis Mallman, creates what she calls 'Italian cuisine with an urban touch'. The

ravioli stuffed with diced lamb covered in rich tomato sauce are as whole-some and tasty as they sound. Also on the menu are inventive sweetcorn tarts, cheese starters and a host of fabulous pasta dishes. Don't bother pick-ing up the wine list: Luciano will pluck a killer bottle out of his cellar for you after he has grilled you about your likes and dislikes. Ask him as many ques-tions as possible about Argentine wine. He's an ex-president of Argentina's Sommelier Association and a wealth of gossip on the Argentine restaurant scene.

Food 8, Service 9, Atmosphere 8

Morena Beach, Costanera Norte, Av. 4899, Costanera

Tel: 4786 0204 / 4788 2521 www.morenabeach.com.ar

Open: daily, noon–4pm, 8pm–closing   AR$75

'*Porteños* built Buenos Aires with their backs to the river' – it's a common
saying here. And it seems to be true: aside from the Yacht Club Argentino
(see Snack), this is the only riverside venue to speak of, so you'll have to put
up with the overpriced, run-of-the-mill seafood, pasta or meat dishes.
Possible River Plate conversation starters could be the scuttling of German
pocket battleship Graf Spey, trying to spot Uruguay on the other side of the
river, or the football team's recent demolition of Boca. Otherwise, just chat
to the staff. They say Morena is where men bring their mistresses and

where celebrities find refuge from the crowds of soap opera fans in the city.
The combination apparently works. Nobody looks at anyone else and those
who fall into neither category are too amazed by the view, and to a certain
extent by Juan Acevedo's menu, to care what is happening around them. The
wine list makes the menu look a little thin, so snack on cookies and milk
before arriving. Morena's pier sits between Jet and Pacha nightclubs, the latter of which takes decadence to another level.

Food 7, Service 7, Atmosphere 8

Nihonbashi, Moreno 2095, Congresso

Tel: 4951 7381

Open: 2.30–11pm. Closed Mondays.

Nihonbashi ('bridge over the river') is a shoes-off, aprons-on, Japanese lager, all chopsticks-in-the-casserole-pan kind of establishment, frequented mainly by the Japanese community. The fact that only a few non-Japanese Argentines tip up at Nihonbashi indicates that sushi is arguably just a fashion statement in Buenos Aires. Come here for perhaps the most authentic

Japanese cuisine in the city and group cook your *sukiyaki* – spring onions, noodles, cabbage and thinly sliced beef – before dipping it in a light soy sauce broth housed in a casserole pan heated by your table's per-

sonal gas stove. For the boys: yes, Nobuhiko Nakatsukasa's wife Naoko – who manages the restaurant – will let you to play with the samurai swords. For the girls: you can play footsie – with no shoes on – under the floating tables. Footwear must be taken off outside your private bamboo encaged space, hand-made by Mr Nakatsukasa, who also prepares the sushi. When booking a table at Nihonbashi, ask for the Umé room (which seats four) and when ordering ask the finest waitresses in Buenos Aires for a Nihonbashi mix of sushi followed by the sukiyaki. *Oishii!* (delicious!).

Food 8, Service 9/10, Atmosphere 7

Olsen, Gorriti 5870, Palermo Hollywood
Tel: 4776 7677
Open: noon–1.30am Tues–Sat; 10am–3pm Sun   AR$70

Aimed at cool-groove locals and Absolut lovers, frequented by both and raved about by food buffs, this Scandinavian-inspired stronghold regularly attracts some of the finest legs, pectorals and egos in the city. There are plenty of carbs on the menu, which doesn't seem to have affected the number of models who surface here, but it is beginning to pull in one tourist too many for our liking, and the food sometimes struggles for consistency. However, that was always inevitable; you don't come here for the food anyway. Olsen's aeroplane hanger-like structure echoes with the sound of chinking vodka glasses and the hum of Argentines gossiping over the chill-out mix; on Sundays the salmon and scrambled eggs – a brunch classic – halt the chattering for at least the odd instant. Behind you, the barmen project an air of attractive superiority and, given that vodka seems to go with anything, they love to freestyle. If you need somewhere a little more

romantic, the restaurant is fronted by a leafy little knoll. This garden area also accommodates day beds ideal for pre-dinner drinks or lunch.

Food 7, Service 7, Atmosphere 9

Osaka, Soler 5608, Palermo Hollywood
Tel: 4775 6964 www.osakafusion.com
Open: 12.30–4pm, 8pm until late. Closed Sundays.   AR$100

This corner fortress in Palermo Hollywood is renowned for pulling in the big 'Don Juans' and the plastic surgery brigade looking for expense accounts. But more importantly the presence of this Peruvian–Japanese fusion shows how Buenos Aires has moved up a couple of rungs in the culinary ranks: Osaka would not seem out of place in Miami, where unnecessarily complicated fusions are still seen as cool. Because the word 'fusion' is still slightly new to Buenos Aires, the flavours are not overlaboured or drowned at Osaka. Rather, this is the finest example of combination cooking in Buenos Aires, and Osaka makes Miami's hip Sushi Samba look ordinary at best. The *ceviche* starters melt in your mouth, the exquisite sushi menu includes fresh tuna – as opposed to, shockingly, the tinned tuna served elsewhere – while the *tempuras*, woks and spicy duck or octopus main courses will have you in a hot flush by pudding time. Either sit at the bar downstairs for a nibble, or let the stunning maître'd from

Cordoba escort you upstairs to enjoy a sofa table. Osaka, which opened here in 2005, has branched out into San Isidro and Punta Del Este. Take this as a sign that Osaka is fashionable, expensive and a safe bet for a pleasurable evening.

Food 9, Service 8, Atmosphere 9/10

Oviedo, Beruti 2602, Palermo

Tel: 4821 3741 / 4822 5415 www.oviedoresto.com.ar
Open: daily, noon–4pm, 8pm–1am   AR$100

Egg specialist Martin Rebaudino will tell you that if you leave an egg in water at 63 degrees for two hours, it will be in exactly the same state as it was after two minutes. Fascinating stuff. All the water has to be exactly the same temperature, however, otherwise a chain reaction will take place and the

egg will be overcooked. Yoking aside, this is unquestionably Buenos Aires' finest Iberian restaurant and arguably for food in general. Rebaudino and Ramón Chiliguay make this place special, as does the dining room cellar, which bulges with European imports – mainly from Spain – as well as wine from Argentina's most private vineyards. The cod, sea bass and sole are all cooked with flair and are accompanied by a variety of vegetables and rich, local sauces. The setting has a wooden, leather-upholstered, hunting-lodge feel, although modern art has replaced the stags' heads and deer antlers, while the clientele comprises older, richer gourmets who shy away from Buenos Aires' sushi houses. Don't expect a fashion parade. This is an intimate restaurant for foodies and those of you interested in eggs.

Food 9/10, Service 9/10, Atmosphere 7

Patagonia Sur, Rocha 801 esq. Pedro de Mendoza, La Boca

Tel: 4303 5917/18 www.restaurantepatagoniasur.com
Open: daily, noon–4pm, 8pm–midnight   AR$80

Francis Mallman is probably Argentina's favourite chef and apparently one of the city's finest lovers – and to be honest, he's shown some balls in building a restaurant right in the heartbeat of Boca, an area famous for tango and the most excitable football fans in the game. Heavily policed in the tourist streets, La Boca is safe to walk through during the day, but is not recommended for nocturnal sightseeing. It is, however, worth getting to Patagonia Sur for dinner, even if it means risking your taxi being hijacked. This is an exquisite example of Argentine cuisine in an in-the-trenches area overlooking the pungent waters of La Boca's docks. But Mallman, who lives above the

restaurant, could put his restaurant banner anywhere in the city and the Argentinos would still stroll in. *Empanadas* and *chori-pan* (*chorizo* in bread), followed by either rib-eye steak or Patagonian lamb – all Argentine staples – comprise the menu. But it's the incorporation of fruit and vegetables to go with the Argentine basics that make Patagonia Sur La Boca's only real dinner candidate. Leave El Obrero (see Snack) for lunch.

Food 9, Service 8, Atmosphere 7

Piegari, Posadas 1042, La Recova, Recoleta
Tel: 4326 9654/9430
Open: daily, noon–3.30pm, 7.30pm–1am   AR$100

Against-the-clock motorists zoom in and out of the city above you as your pasta boils. La Recova is the sub-motorway restaurant strip beside the Four Seasons hotel. The diverse mix of restaurants contains, among others, ex-Boca Juniors coach Carlos Bianchi's eclectic Bond restaurant with its soap-opera crowd, and Piegari, the pick of the bunch. Attracting a similar bunch of

well-to-do families, surgically enhanced, diamond-encrusted Argentines and illicit lovers as the other restaurants, Pieragi delivers an ambitious, consistent and extremely flavoursome Italian menu. The pasta dishes are huge and made for sharing, filled with juicy and wholesome fillings and made with bundles of Latin passion. The *sorrentinos* (ravioli-style pasta) come with rich cheese or tomato sauces and are almost too filling, but can be washed down with fabulous wines from the comprehensive wine list.

Food 9, Service 8, Atmosphere 7

Resto, Montevideo 938, Recoleta
Tel: 4816 6711
Open: noon–3pm Mon–Fri (8–11pm Thurs–Fri). Closed weekends.

This is the kind of place you go to tell your partner you plan to marry the transvestite you met at Transformations (see Party), or to inform your family that you have decided to emigrate to Paraguay and will never return. They will understand. The white walls and quiet ambient music allow for intense conversation, much to the delight of the burning ears of the waitresses, who continually top up your water as soon as the topic heats up. Resto is about

food (try the king prawns followed by duck and then the chocolate pudding), a gripping exchange and excellent service. Open from Thursdays onwards in the evenings, the restaurant is highly respected among Buenos Aires' top restaurateurs such as Tomo Uno's manager Frederico (see page 95), who judges restaurants purely on their kitchen, and not their image. Resto is a strange sort of place: set in a stark, canteen-styled room at the back of the Central Architect's Society's arcade, it is reminiscent of a museum cafeteria. When you finally emerge, don't be tempted by the Jack the Ripper bar in front of the arcade; head instead to Milion (see Drink), just down the road, for a pitstop Martini on the mansion steps.

Food 9, Service 10, Atmosphere 5

Santa Gula, Jorge Newbery 3902 (Corner of Guevara), Colegiales
Tel: 4552 4599   AR$50
Open: 11am–3pm, 8pm–1.30am. Closed Saturdays, Sundays and Mondays.

If you're looking for somewhere to lose yourself among the wide boulevards of Buenos Aires, try Santa Gula; fittingly, it is the favourite restaurant of Juan Estrada, Argentina's top landscaped labyrinth designer. The taxi ride out to Colegiales (on the dodgy side of Cordoba Avenue) can be a little disconcerting, but on the corner of Jorge Newbery and Guevara, Santa Gula offers a break from the Buenos Aires *histericismo* scene. The French china, the open kitchen and the nearby bus station all seem to clash, but bind together to form a chirpy *barrio* atmosphere. That typical Buenos Aires phrase *buena onda* ('good vibes') fits well here. We recommend the

chilled *ceviche* soup, the mini fondue or tapas selections to start, and the breaded chicken fingers or ricotta *crêpes* for a main course. And while the wine list is not extensive – more middle of the range plonks than exclusive *bodegas* – Santa Gula sends out the message that its little love affair, albeit removed from the tourist track, is working because of its neighbourhood, freshly cut flowers ambience. And you are actually still within striking distance of Palermo Hollywood. Just head over a railway bridge and through a few back streets and you're back in affluent civilization. Arrive early, eat some fondue, inhale some bus fumes, talk communism for a couple of hours and leave satisfied

Food 7, Service 8, Atmosphere 8

Sirop, Vicente López 1661 Local 11, Pasaje del Correo, Recoleta

Tel: 4813 5900 www.siroprestaurant.com
Open: daily, noon–3.30pm, 8pm–midnight (12.30am Fri–Sat)   AR$85

A cheeky little dinner date special in Recoleta, where the all-female management make San Francisco restaurateurs look bone idle. Passionate about their lamb, their wine and their intimate, candlelit atmosphere, the Sirop crowd are protective of their culture, so toss out that short-sleeved shirt that should never have come with you in the first place and dress elegantly. Sirop's creator and Chef Liliana Numer who was taught to make puddings

at Le Nôtre cooking school in Paris – produces some of the fanciest, albeit richest dishes in Recoleta. The puddings, as you would expect, will have your teeth rotting by coffee time, and the wine list matches the menu's bold flavours, such as Liliana's duck *à la cassis* special. In fact, intentionally or not, most of the food here is particularly rich and sweet. The not-so-sweet Nectarine, which serves French cuisine next door, is also popular with locals. Do not confuse Sirop with Sirop Folie across the alleyway.

Food 8, Service 9, Atmosphere 7

Standard, Guatemala y Fitz Roy, Palermo Hollywood
Tel: 4779 2774
Open: noon–3.30pm, 8.30pm–1am. Closed Sundays.   AR$75

Mothers cook comfort food for a reason, being so wholesome, healthy and tasty the family will come round to visit them again and again. The Standard offers a deluxe version of comfort food, with calf-brain ravioli, crab cakes and salmon *tartare* on the menu to go with the cocktails – not that mothers are in the habit of offering you Cosmopolitans. Another winner from the owners of Sudestada (see page 93), which sits on the opposite corner packed with Asian food enthusiasts, the Standard has simpler offerings of meat or fish accompanied by vegetables. Yes, vegetables – something of a novelty in Buenos Aires. Standard's bare, simple but stylish 1950s-look diner

has been given a pristine modern makeover in an attempt to make this restaurant all about the food. And it is. The clientele are now drawn to the duck pie, the shoe-box sized beef on the bone and Standard's trendy minimalist vibe. This is homely cuisine with attitude, served in a chic Palermo Hollywood setting.

Food 8/9, Service 7/8, Atmosphere 7

Sucre, Sucre 676, Belgrano

Tel: 4782 9082   www.sucrerestaurant.com.ar
Open: daily, noon–4pm, 8pm–2am   AR$95

Pinch yourself. Am I really in South America? This could be New York. On a Wednesday evening book a late table at Sucre before heading to Rumi for drinks and a dance (see Party). You will leave having sampled one of the largest cellars in the city, which sits, quite inconspicuously, in the middle of

this hip, industrial, bomb-shelter space. With the same net of owners as Bar Uriarte (see page 70) and El Diamante (see Drink), you are guaranteed high-end style at Sucre, and while most concierges send their foreign guests here, Sucre continues to lure Buenos Aires' trendsetters as well. Head chef Fernando Trocca gives Sucre the edge over her sister restaurants as far as the food is concerned, but when you cross the bridge above the bar and survey the scene, you will appreciate also its understated finesse. For the at-the-coal-face Sucre experience book a table beside the kitchen, where pigs are being spit-roasted and an army of sous-chefs, led by Gonzálo Sacot, passionately chop away and squeeze their sauce bottles over their pans. If you do fancy heading to Rumi afterwards (it's just around the corner), ask for a table beside the window at one of the sofas, highly reminiscent of Bar Uriarte, for a little calm before the storm.

Food 8, Service 7, Atmosphere 8

Sudestada, Guatemala 5602, Palermo Hollywood
Tel: 4776 3777
Open: noon–3pm and 8pm–late. Closed Sundays.   AR$65

A Sudestada is the sudden rotation of cold southern winds to the south-east, otherwise known as the South Eastern Hit. Sudestada the restaurant has been serving spicy South East Asian dishes since opening in 1999 from

its Palermo Hollywood cornershop hideout. Always packed, *porteños*, who are gradually realising the delights of spicy red, yellow or green curries, either get their chilli kick here or at Green Bamboo (see page 78). Fusions are out of the question, it's straight down the line Thai, Vietnamese,

Cambodian or Malaysian. Founded by entrepreneurs Estanis Carenzo, Leonardo Azulay and Pablo Giúdice, who have recently opened another branch in Madrid. Much of Sudestada's popularity comes down to the fabulous starters, from which we recommend you choose a tapas style selection. But it's the brimming corner shop ambience (capacity for only 38 covers) overlooked by the chefs and the cocktail shakers that make Sudestada one of Palermo Hollywood firm favourites, and one of the only unpretentious places in BA to get ones spice fix.

Food 9, Service 7, Atmosphere 9

Thymus, Lerma 525, Villa Crespo

Tel: 4772 1936   www.thymusrestaurant.com.ar   AR$75
Open: from 8pm Mon–Fri; 11.30am–4pm, 8pm–late Sat; 11.30am–6pm Sun

Thymus is one of the undervalued gems of the BA dinner scene; excellent food in a sophisticated, arty setting, shielded from the crowds by Cordoba Avenue and complemented by 878, a speakeasy of a bar a few blocks away. Martin Vergara's timeless stone sculptures are scattered around Thymus. Unsurprisingly, since daughter Maria runs a gallery on the first floor and

oversees Thymus the restaurant below, where chef Fernando Mayoral, trained by Michel Bras, creates excellent duck, quail, chicken and beef dishes in his adopted *estilo Francés*. Deep flavours and an innate understanding of produce lead to astonishingly delicious masterpieces. The setting, an unpretentious space with wooden floors, black tables and stone sculptures, is only slightly tarnished by the presence of canned soft drinks, but Alberto, the sommelier, will smooth things over by recommending a fabulous bottle of Argentine *tinto*. Thymus is starting to pull in a hefty A-list dinership, so book ahead for the table by the fireplace.

Food 9, Service 8/9, Atmosphere 7/8

Tomo Uno, Carlos Pellegrini 521, Centre

Tel: 4326 6695/6698

Open: noon–3pm, 7.30pm–1am Mon–Fri; 8pm–midnight   AR$120

In 1971 sisters Ada and Ebe Concaro opened Tomo Uno in the district of Belgrano, just north of Palermo. In 1980 Ada won a Golden Spoon for her efforts, and the Tomo Uno we now know shifted downtown to the Panamericano Hotel in 1993. To be honest, the two go together as well as turnips and olives: one of Buenos Aires' most sophisticated restaurants housed in one of Buenos Aires' largest (albeit stylish) hotels, which sits beside the obelisk in the centre of Capital Federal. However, somehow this seemingly star-crossed alliance manages to work. Tomo Uno is highly rated among Argentina's top chefs, primarily because of the flavour-filled rabbit, pheasant, duck and lamb dishes. The Patagonian lamb, in particular, is as

tender as you will find in Buenos Aires. The message hot from the kitchen is that the food represents 'sophisticated experimentation, without the unnecessary fashionable and exotic extras with which so many restaurants tart up their menus'. Ada's son Federico, the manager, will recommend a bottle of Quimera – a Malbec, Merlot, Cabernet Sauvignon and Franc blend – to accompany the lamb. Come here for the food, but not the rather reposed atmosphere.

Food 9, Service 9, Atmosphere 6

drink...

Argentines like a bit of everything in moderation, and that includes alcohol. European-style binge drinking is unheard of; instead their efforts are poured into attracting and enticing the opposite sex.

The BA drinking scene is split into three factions. First, the out-and-out bar, frequented before heading out to a nightclub. Carnal, Congo and Mundo Bizarro, all in Palermo Viejo, are perfect club warm-ups, or just as good for a few simple cocktails.

Then there is the sophisticated restaurant/bar, which is commonplace in Buenos Aries. Since they are an international concept, they go down well with the fashionable *porteños* who love anything non-Argentine. Casa Cruz, El Gran Bar Danzon, Kansas (Avenida del Libertador 4625, tel: 4776 4100) and Rubia y Negra are all restaurants for those looking to enjoy a quick dinner and then a mingle. 678 (right), an ex-private member's club, is possibly the most glamorous location in town. The more down to earth Kandi and Soul Café are the pick of Las Cañitas' strip bars on Báez Street.

Lastly, there is the underground bar culture, where a knock on the door, the press of a buzzer and/or a password are necessary. A few minutes' walk from Palermo Viejo on the rougher side of Córdoba Avenue, 878 is the most mainstream of the bunch, while Puerta Uno in Belgrano is our favourite. The gay-friendly Kim y Novak also loves its underground vibe, and is probably the naughtiest of the lot. One gritty underground wildcard is Salón Pueyrredón (Santa Fe 4560), where it's best to turn up at 6am – and remember to hide your wallet and anything valuable.

For warming down the night and going on until midday, El Alamo in Recoleta is a more relaxed choice if an after-hours rave (see Party) feels like a bridge too far at 6.30am.

For pool sharks, we have strategically selected three options through the city: Gibraltar in San Telmo, Deep Blue in Recoleta and finally the latest branch of Tazz in Palermo Viejo, which sits right in Buenos Aires' nocturnal hotspot.

The *porteño* drinking culture is centred on dating. Argentine society is dominated by what men want and what women will allow them to do. Drinks follow dinner only if dinner goes well, which partly explains the surge in restaurant/bars. If a supper invitation has been refused, then a drink after the young lady has had dinner with her family is the next best thing.

At weekends, Argentine men tend to drink beer (usually Quilmes) and talk about women and football at home before heading to a bar or a nightclub to meet the opposite sex. Note that Argentine men pay for everything and with the rise in tourism, bars have become too expensive for those who earn pesos, limiting the number of men who go to bars. Argentine girls have similar habits, in that they get together with their *amigas* (girlfriends), usually over a glass of diet coke and a pack

of cigarettes, and chat about the men they have been subjecting to mental torture before heading out to be bought drinks all night.

The terms '*salir a bailar*' (go out to dance) and '*salir a tomar algo*' (go out for a drink) signify different things. To '*salis a tomar algo*' probably means going on a date, while if you '*salis a bailar*' it will be with a group of friends.

The drinking scene in Buenos Aires is thus sculpted for style, sex and meeting the love of your life, rather than alcoholic indulgence. Policemen are kept busier dealing with car thefts and riots rather than hordes of inebriated locals.

647, Tacuarí 647, San Telmo

Tel: 4331 3026
Open: 8pm to closing. Closed Mondays from 8pm.

When Englishmen Terry Walshe and Nick Hargreaves opened 647 as a members-only club in 2006, the number of cosmetic enhancements in Buenos Aires went through the roof. Everybody wanted to become part of the San Telmo flea-pit transformed into a futuristic palace, styled in what

they call 'Shanghai opulence' – until, that is, the small matter of the AR$2,000 membership fee reared its head. In their enthusiasm, Walshe and Hargreaves had overlooked the fact that fashionable Argentines, the kind who give prestige to a place like this, do not and will not pay for anything. They consider their presence payment enough. So the membership fee was scrapped, and 647 is now open to anyone who can afford the drinks. Two factors make 647 different from other high-roller bars: first, the design is as unique as you will witness in Buenos Aires; and second, the bar is run by Tato (see Play for his cocktail classes) who, along with Casa Cruz' Ines (see page 102), is the finest bartender in the city. Wednesday nights attract a late crew of models and their coiffured chaperones, en route to Asia de Cuba, but Friday nights are most popular. Currently misfiring but potentially brilliant, 647 is still the most impressive place to twiddle your olive stick and should be high on your list.

878, Thames 878, Villa Crespo/Palermo Viejo
Tel: 4773 1098
Open: daily, from 10pm

Bar 878 is one of those 'ring-the-doorbell' hideouts, playing the role of the speakeasy bar disguised from the prohibition police. However, the state-of-the-art cash till is an obvious giveaway – 878 is an above-board business and actually one of the more sanitized bars for a late-night get-together in this part of town. The building, formerly a carpenter's workshop, hosts upwards of 50 drinkers, all revelling in the bar's 'hidden' image. Crucially, 878 stays open during January, which has ensured it a dedicated following of cocktail fanatics who quench their thirst here throughout the year. The highly skilled barmen impress the most fervent cocktail addicts with their own concoc-

tions (although steer clear of their 'Fernet Branca' peppered vodka and peach mix). Dine at Thymus, follow with cocktails at 878 and then head on for beers at Mundo Bizarro. If you're still standing by 3am and make it to Podesta or Club Niceto nightclubs, and finish off the morning at La Conzuelo for an after-party.

El Alamo, Uruguay 1175–77, (entrance on Av. Santa Fe and Arenales), Recoleta
Tel: 4813 7324
Open: daily, 24 hours

Intriguingly, the Argentine press have labelled El Alamo 'an elegant stately-home bar'. By this, however, it would seem they mean bikini contests, free drinks for girls (until midnight) and all-day drinking sessions, so if you're expecting British aristocrats in tweeds you might be a little disappointed. Feel free to take your clothes off, tie them around your head and dance on the bar – Ukrainian barman Antony would be offended if you didn't. He's normally as inebriated as the rest of the Alamo crew, who spend most of

their off-duty hours propping up the bar. Just don't hide their clothes, or they won't let you choose the music. This is Buenos Aires' only real 24-hour beer pit, the only one in which smoking is ignored; here, you can enjoy Recoleta's finest bikini contest, held on the first floor on Sunday, Monday and Tuesday nights. The establishment was formerly 'Shoeless Joe's' until 2006, when it became 'Shoeless Joe's El Alamo', named after (yep, you guessed it!) the Alamo. El Alamo's ground floor is slightly dark, but a devoted ex-pat following turns up for the cheap whisky, 4-litre jugs of beer – the largest in Buenos Aires – and rock music that shakes the shot glasses all night long.

El Dorrego, Defensa 1098, San Telmo
Tel: 4361 0141
Open: daily, 8am–3am

People have been sipping ale at El Dorrego's bar for over a century. Carve your lover's name on the bar while he orders the beers, soak up the tango culture in front of San Telmo's most famous market-place and don't complain if your Quilmes (beer) is not topped up to the line. This is old-school San Telmo, where men used to wrap their legs around one another as the tango dances were developed. El Dorrego is as touristy as an airport lounge,

but still manages to pull off the authenticity the wood panelling and pastel
yellow walls exude. Pop along to the Sunday market in the plaza and reflect
on how you were talked into buying your boyfriend that bead necklace he
always wanted, then contemplate dinner at La Brigada or Pentanque.

Buda Bar, Olga Cossettini 1051, Puerto Madero
Tel: 4893 9500 www.buda-bar.com.ar
Open: daily, noon–late

Following on from Asia de Cuba's lead, Buda Bar brings meditation to
Buenos Aires' docklands. As you might expect, Buddha statues and lollipop
Indian lampshades adorn this brand-new dockhouse space, which overlooks
Puerto Madero's touristy restaurants and muddy water. The Buda Bar
initially captured the imagination of the Argentines, pulling in an attractive
vodka/karma crowd, but at the time of writing a pleasant late-evening

sharpener on a Wednesday or Thursday is as much as we can guarantee; however, this could all change for the better. Whether it's full or not, Buda Bar's restaurant/bar/lounge format is a proven concept in Buenos Aires, and should provide dockland fun, but if you're not convinced you can always try the White Club and Asia de Cuba just down the road.

El Carnal, Niceto Vega 5511, Palermo Viejo
Tel: 4772 7582
Open: 9pm–3am (4.30am Thurs–Sat). Closed Sundays and Mondays.

Dutchmen – renowned for their mid-week drinking and protracted week-ends – love Carnal for its legendary Thursday night belters – pre-Club 69 get-togethers on the stargazing deck, which is heaving with 20-somethings and has been for the last five years. The flickering green flames over the

front door give just a hint of what's to come. Inside, El Carnal's cool, slightly trashy décor exudes a trailer-park vibe, while the roof terrace, which gives the bar the 'car-nality', hums with the sexiest stargazers en route to Club Niceto, where Thursday night's Club 69 party had historically been held (see Party). El Carnal seldom fails to fill, and despite the news that the Club 69 party has moved from Club Niceto to Roxy, just around the corner, the bar continues to throb with *porteños* and in-the-know out-of-towners.

Casa Cruz, Uriarte 1658, Palermo Viejo
Tel: 4823 1112 www.casa-cruz.com
Open: 8.30pm–2am. Closed Sundays.

Savvy locals will tell you this restaurant-cum-bar is the place to be seen. To a certain extent it is, luring BA's wealthiest clients in through its storey-high golden gates, as well as high-goal polo players and their patrons, sugar daddies and a healthy supply of dollar-loving blondes. The palatial feel gives Casa Cruz the 'wow' factor, but the reality is that the demand for the restaurant grew too fast for the kitchen to deliver. Despite a well-designed

menu, many diners leave disappointed having spent a fortune – not that they would admit it. Which is why we recommend Casa Cruz for an early (11.30pm) drink, particularly on a Thursday night, rather than dining here. From behind the solid, oval-shaped bar, Ines – the city's celebrity bartender – has forged one of the longest cocktail lists in town, so study it carefully and don't blow your cover and ask her to invent something to suit your taste. Being cool at Casa Cruz means flashing your cash, tipping well and taking no notice of the steely glares you receive from the studs and *diosas* (goddesses) around you.

La Cigale, 25 de Mayo 722, Retiro
Tel: 4312 8275
Open: 6pm–late. Closed Sundays.

Head to La Cigale for Tuesday night's 'Soirée Française'. Not because it's French, but because other Tuesday night options in Buenos Aires are limited. The long, dark bar is decorated with baskets of pineapples and oranges (used for daquiris) and illuminated in sordid red. La Cigale is neither hip nor stylish; instead the somewhat grubby bar pulsates with electronic beats and a gritty alcohol and cocaine charged 20-something crowd. Packed in like sardines, drinkers are often left waiting at the bar for what seems like hours, so order a strong drink or two and relax into the vibe. Dadá is your pre-La

Cigale warm-up bar on a Tuesday, while on a Wednesday La Cigale itself works as a warm-up to Bahrein, the nightclub with a bank-vault VIP lounge (see Party).

Congo, Honduras 5329, Palermo Viejo
Tel: 4833 5857
Open: 8pm–3.30pm. Closed Mondays.

The great thing about Congo is the outside terrace. Although you can perch on a chair in the corridor bar – allegedly the longest in the area – and knock back your 25-peso cocktail as stunning Argentine divas and mani-cured polo players strut past, you'd be wise to follow them through to the

garden terrace, which, it has to be said, is the finest al-fresco social-climbing spot in the city – let alone Palermo Viejo. The leafy patio has a summer pub vibe where – abnormally for Buenos Aires – you can chat without having to shout. Inside, the more upbeat brown and beige chill-out lounge is filled with the latest in contemporary beats. From October to December Congo will be top of most people's list, so arrive before 11pm having grabbed a bite at Desde El Alma or Dominga (see Eat). If, after you've had your fill of people-watching, you feel like something a little less mainstream, Kim Y Novak should be next on the list (see page 109).

Dadá, San Martin 941, Micro Centro
Tel: 4314 4787
Open: noon–3am. Closed Sundays.

Like the art, Dadá could be described as a random collation from every day life, but here it's people rather than things: businessmen winding down,

tourists who have lost their way and loafers who pretend they have been working all day. With Pop Art covering the walls – mostly enormous Lichtensteins – and a glitterball hanging from the ceiling, regulars choose Dadá because it's a world away from the breakneck speed of life in the Micro Centro. The barmen, serious professionals, take pride in massaging away the knots of the stressed *porteño* with a glass full of gin graced with the merest splash of tonic. Dadá is a good choice for an afternoon/early evening drink, but also consider the Downtown double on a Tuesday night: head to Dadá at around 10pm before rolling on to grittier La Cigale. Dadá is the queen in the Downtown beehive and superior to the Kilkenny and Downtown Mattias, about which you will have been misinformed.

Deep Blue, Ayacucho 1240, Recoleta
Tel: 4827 4415 www.deepblue.com.ar
Open: daily, 6pm–4am

Pour yourself another beer from your private lager tap while the loser racks up; order nibbles from the friendly team of waitresses; and bet a few greenbacks on a frame or two – with few pool sharks in Buenos Aires you stand a decent chance avoiding a Paul Newman 'hustler', providing you clarify the rules before the break. Argentines have added on a few cheeky footnotes of their own to the classic pool regulations, with pot the black in the same pocket as your last stripe or colour being the most basic. Private drinking booths line Deep Blue's ground floor and additional tables are

housed on the first floor, but stick to the main room if you can. Deep Blue is not all about pool, though. For those not up for a frame, the sofa booths are languid enough for a few leisurely drinks while the garden terrace is reputedly frequented by hot male Columbian dancers (if that's your thing). The music ranges from Madonna to Deep Dish to Reggaeton: *un toque de todo* (a little bit of everything).

El Diamante, Malabia 1688, Palermo Viejo
Tel: 4831 5735
Open: noon–2am. Closed Sundays.

A cold beer while watching the sun go down over Palermo Viejo's rooftops is hard to beat. The first *porteños* were lured to El Diamante by Fernando Trocca's Latin American cuisine, then the secret of El Diamante's roof terrace leaked out during the Palermo Viejo revolution, and 'that restaurant above the boutique shop' became known as the killer *terraza* bar above a restaurant with a famous chef. Mid-afternoon aperitifs at the weekend will restore any thirsty shopper, while the more intimate late-evening beverage with intoxicated Mexican artists and off-duty bartenders is the highlight for El Diamante fans, particularly on a Monday night. Steer clear of the cocktails at the bar when the terrace gets packed, as there's no sign of a

shaker and (perhaps quite refreshingly) not an olive in sight.

Gibraltar, Penap 895, San Telmo

Tel: 4362 5310
Open: daily, 6pm–4am

Gibraltar, or 'hibraltar' as it is pronounced, is as close to an English public house as you will find in Buenos Aires. No, you're quite right – you didn't come to BA to drink ale in English pub surroundings; but justify this outing to Gibraltar with the lure of the bar's original Pacman machine, pool table and the fact that San Telmo is not really a chichi bar hotspot. So if you are fancy an early evening pint you might as well do it properly, at Gibraltar, which comes complete with pint glasses, seriously hot curry, pub loos and a resident dog that walks around waiting to lap up the spillage. The owner also owns Bangalore Pub and curry house around the corner from Carnal in Palermo Viejo. Up there you don't need an English pub. Down here in San Telmo, however, Gibraltar is a godsend.

El Gran Danzon, Libertad 1161, Recoleta
Tel: 4811 1108 www.granbardanzon.com.ar
Open: 7pm–late Mon–Fri; 8pm–late Sat–Sun

With open breezeblock faces, a speckled, light slate bar, an all-imported liquor cabinet and an affluent wine list, this was the bar to be seen in 2003. The Danzon's bomb-shelter feel carried the New York vibe, and wealthy *porteños* and ex-pats would come to dine here before standing up to mingle and sip Johnny Black. A few years on and the Danzon continues to fill, albeit with an older, less refined selection of *compadres* than before. However, this remains the most sophisticated of Recoleta's bars and you can smell the

scented candles from half a block away. The small entrance is found on Libertad street, where you march up the stairs past candles and the bouncer. The lab-coated bartenders stand tall behind their Martini shakers, and mix cocktails with fabulous precision. Turn up at around 11.30pm for drinks after the resident DJ arrives, or book the sofa section for dinner. While the salmon, sushi and beef main courses are all delicious, bear in mind that after the main kitchen is closed, the Danzon still offers fabulously tasty chicken pesto sandwiches until closing-time.

Kandi, Báez 340, Las Cañitas
Tel: 4772 2453
Open: 8.30pm–4am. Closed Mondays.

If you arrive mid-week in Buenos Aires, Kandi will get the blood flowing. Imagine a duplex apartment with the bedroom overlooking the living area, make it about 20 times bigger, pimp it out with decadent lighting, play

Victoria's Secret catwalk videos on the cinema screen, add in two well-manned bars downstairs, fill the place with a horde of young, beautiful *porteñas* and a few handsome Argentine men, and hire a DJ to get the pro-

ceedings moving. Food is an option at this Las Cañitas candy shop, but don't expect an excellent dining experience: the music is far too loud for a civilized supper, and the sushi is average at best. Few will care, however – because after all, it's all about the look. Kandi

is as close to a nightclub as you will get without it being a nightclub: a pleasant medium/fast-paced bar for the hard-hitting, hip traveller.

Kim y Novak, Guemes 4900, Palermo Viejo
Tel: 4773 7521
Open: 9.30pm–late. Closed Mondays.

Kim y Novak prides itself on its transvestite, lesbian and drug-dealer clientele. In truth, the only transvestites here are the waiters, and luckily they do look like men – in Argentina you can be fooled thanks to an army of cosmetic surgeons and a bit of will power. Kim y Novak says 'I'm an

underground bar, only come here if you are gay, want to score some coke or you're looking for a little bit of trouble.' That's something of an exaggeration: the tranny waiters are just for show, and the bar attracts a friendly mixture of gay, straight and open-minded girls – although the loo seats are, indeed, rather dusty. Kim y Novak is best enjoyed down-

109

stairs where pretty, fittingly arrogant waitresses (proud that they work in an alternative kind of bar) serve ferocious cocktails with attitude, up-and-coming DJs regularly spin and the low sofas and cushioned slabs are mighty comfortable, yet easy to get out of if you are stalked by a bearded Mr Sister. Definitely a late-night bar, so don't even dream of pitching up before 1am.

Milión, Parana 1048, Recoleta

Tel: 4815 9925 www.milionargentina.com.ar
Open: noon–2am (3am Thurs, 4am Fri); 7.30pm–4am Sat; 8pm–2am Sun

Think the Cabaña room in Los Angeles, but without the movie stars. Milión has long been considered Recoleta's most impressive bar; the 20th-century mansion building provides a super-seductive setting to sip on a dirty Martini. Tourists have cottoned on to this, however, and Milión is no longer the protected national park it used to be. In the evenings the bar is now flooded

with visitors from all over the world, so avoid peak hours if it's an all-Argentine climate you seek – pre-dinner drinks or cocktails at 1am before heading out are probably the best decision. Ignore your instincts and don't be tempted to eat in the ground-floor garden – Resto is just down the road for proper food (see Eat). Milión is best viewed from the first-floor bar, where tattooed, slightly camp bartenders ply their trade. Despite the influx of tourists, Argentines still love Milión, and this will always be Recoleta's – if not Buenos Aires' – most aesthetically pleasing watering-hole.

Mott, El Salvador, Palermo Viejo

Tel: 4685 4833 / 4306
Open: daily, 9am–late

At Mott, stick to late afternoon/early evening drinks and a spot of people-watching. Its wide-open façade on Palermo Viejo's El Salvador street is an inviting location for cool-off cocktails after a credit-card bashing session in

the area's boutique shops. In addition to a gourmet menu nibbles are available, so treat Mott as a pitstop before heading back to the hotel. For those with an hour or two to kill, you couldn't do much better than observing Buenos Aires' trend-setters strut by. Mott opened in late 2006, and as yet is without a loyal band of regulars, but its location, airy minimalist style and well-trained bar staff are already attracting fans. Easily accessible from the street, Mott will never be an exclusive, hip bar, but because it is indispensable to shopaholics, it will undoubtedly be here for the foreseeable future.

Mundo Bizarro, Serrano 1222, Palermo Viejo

Tel: 4773 1967 www.mundobizarrobar.com
Open: daily, 9pm–close

Mundo Bizarro moved locations in 2006 but has brought its trademark giant flying insect with it. This is the new version of Mundo Bizarro, or 'Bizarro' as locals fondly call it. Bettie Page comic book pictures, red vinyl diner booths, wacky cocktails and an up-for-it band of regulars characterized the last venue; the 2006 version is bigger and always packed with a mixture of hip Americans and genuinely fashionable Argentines, with bathrooms daubed in

Rat Fink graffiti. Better? No, just more crowded, more commercial and slightly darker.

Alongside Congo, this is one bar that will always be full, will stay open until 5am and where Pablo the manager will take enormous care over your cocktail, irrespective of how many thirsty sailors are waiting in front of him. If you fancy something a little more rustic, however, 878 is within walking distance, on Thames street.

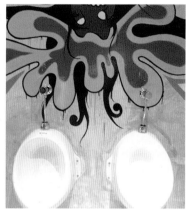

Puerta Uno, Juramento 1667, Belgrano
Tel: 4706 1522
Open: daily, 9.30pm–5am (depending on how busy it is)

You score many a Brownie point for darkening this doorstep. Puerta Uno is the underground bar in a dark Belgrano street that nobody likes to talk about. There are a number of reasons for this: firstly, people come here because they love to think of Puerta Uno as a secret bar available only to those good-looking or trendy enough to know the owners, Marcelo and Robertiño. Secondly, the cocktails are some of the most nurtured in the city – sake and fruit concoctionos are the barman's speciality – and at AR$15 are just expensive enough to make the bar hip but not overpriced. Thirdly,

the DJ mixes club classics with tasteful rock tracks, allowing the refreshingly unpretentious crowd (Belgrano is a down-to-earth neighbourhood next to Palermo Hollywood) to enjoy themselves without pretension. Lastly, Marcelo changes the décor every three months to keep the bar fresh. It helps that his mother leases out stylish bar furniture for parties as a profession and advises on flowers – Peruvian lilies are popular here. Oh, and Robertiño's father, a footballing legend, won the World Cup with Argentina in 1978, which basically categorizes him as royalty. Look for the Harley Davidson motorbike outside the 'hidden' entrance and ask for Robertiño or Marcelo, or you will be denied entry.

Rubia y Negra, Libertad 1630, Recoleta
Tel: 4313 1125
Open: 6pm–2am Mon–Fri; 7pm–3am Sat

Cut from the same cloth as El Gran Bar Danzon (see page 108) and Bar Uriarte (see Eat), Rubia y Negra sits beside Maria Vasquez's boutique store on the first floor of a Recoleta block, a two-minute walk from the Caesar Park, Four Seasons and Hyatt hotels. Really a microbrewery, but disguised as a sleek cocktail lounge, it is ideal for drinks at 10pm or even a quiet dinner during the week. It's situated in a smart Recoleta neighbourhood where many of the regulars head out of the city during the weekend, so Wednesday or Thursday nights are best for the Rubia y Negra experience,

when high-society youths come out to play. While the casks of ale, brewed on site, hang over the bar, the truth is that the beer's just so-so and is more novelty than anything else – you're better off going straight for the wine or cocktails.

The Shamrock, Rodriguez Peña 1220, Recoleta
Tel: 4812 3584
Open: 6pm–late Mon–Fri; 8pm–late Sat–Sun

Of all the Irish bars in BA, the 'Shammy' attracts the more acclimatized ex-pats, as well as the open-minded locals who take pride in welcoming outsiders with open arms. The basement of the Shamrock has seen a resurgence in recent times. What was a dodgy subterranean vault has become a vibrant dance-floor flanked by sofas and headed by a raised bar. Thursdays (from midnight) and the weekend (Fridays and Saturdays from 1am) are all

popular nights for downstairs 'Shammy' action, while the street-level bar usually brims from 10pm onwards.

Soul Café, Báez 246 and Supersoul, Báez 252, Las Cañitas
Tel: 4778 3115 and 4776 3905 (respectively)
Open: daily, 6pm (7pm Sat)–late

The Afro bartenders have been replaced with punk-rock waitresses, but the 1970s retro feel lingers on in this Las Cañitas funk lounge. Soul Café and her neighbouring sister bar, Supersoul, dominate the Báez strip, so split your time between the two before heading to Kandi a block away. The bars really get going from Wednesday night onwards. In 2003 you could get away with having dinner at Soul Café, but nowadays Las Cañitas is just for drinking, so stick to Soul Café's red light zone bar for beers, and tuck your head around the corner to Supersoul for stronger cocktails. If you desperately need to eat, then try the hugely commercial Sushi Club, only a few doors down the

road, before launching your evening from one of the Soul sisters.

Tazz, Armenia 1744, Palermo Viejo

Tel: 4551 5010 www.tazzbars.com

Open: daily, noon–3am (until 6am Fri–Sat)

If Gibraltar is your San Telmo pub, and Deep Blue is your Recoleta pool bar, then Tazz is your Palermo Soho haunt. Snobby Argentines would call Tazz 'una grasada total' (something like 'the tackiest place on Earth'), which it is – but just go with it. The flash art wallpaper will have you feeling enjoyably dizzy by your third frame. Try not to confuse this Tazz with the Plaza Serrano branch: this is the newer version beside Podesta nightclub. Surprisingly, you must call ahead for a table, unless you want a bolshy wait-ress to strike

you down with an 'I-seriously-can't-believe-you-didn't-book' remark. Perfect for post-shopping, or while your partner shops in Palermo Viejo, Tazz also works for a competitive after-dinner frame before you head on to a proper cocktail bar.

snack...

Porteños are snackaholics: '*Nos gusta un poco de todo, pero no en exceso,*' they say, 'We like a bit of everything, but not in excess.'

And what might this mean? A *café con leche* with a croissant in the morning, a sandwich, steak or salad at lunchtime, afternoon tea *à l'anglais*, followed by a light bite on the way back from work, before a late dinner, which is often followed by a late-night *helado* (ice cream).

By enjoying, but not over-indulging in, so many small meals during the day, Argentines manage to maintain not only their heavy social schedules, but their svelte figures as well. This is particularly useful during the summer months when the beaches of Punta del Este beckon, while the thought of walking around in the 35-degree heat on a full stomach also plays a part in the lightness of meals.

Buenos Aires does, however, cater for the more regimented 'three-square-meals-a-day' brigade, and it is perfectly acceptable to settle in for a lazy lunch overlooking the river, docklands or a park, particularly if you are not taking part in the city's rat race.

Snacking is an adventure in Buenos Aires, helped by the fact that taxis are cheap. So, if you are within a 30-block radius of your chosen lunch spot/tea palace/coffee shop and it's not rush hour, it's worth travelling the distance to get a little of what you really want.

For dodgy underground venues, look no further than Providencia (Palermo Hollywood) and El Obrero (La Boca), both of which are gritty but ooze character. At the opposite end of the scale, Gioia at the Palacio Duhau Park Hyatt will not fail to seduce you with palatial buffets.

If lunch under a tree with the River Plate lapping at your feet is more you, then charm your way into the Yacht Club Argentino (below). While you're in Puerto Madero – the dockland area where it's best to eat during the day rather than the evening – try Cabaña Las Lilas, the city's most-popular restaurant with concierges. For a healthier option near the docks, don't forget I Fresh Market.

For tea and cakes, Florencio and Chez Pauline in Recoleta are both secluded little eateries, while Palermo Viejo's Bar 6, also ideal for breakfast, is more of a chic, people-watching place. Oui Oui (Palermo Hollywood), on the other hand, brings gossiping with the girls over a slice of cake to another level.

Moving on to places where real *porteños* hang out in their *barrio*, Voulez Bar is great for a late lunch in Palermo, while the close by Museo de Evita and Croque Madame are two of our favourites.

In the air-conditioned pizzeria category the Avenida del Libertador branch of Pizza Cero pulls in a young, fashionable crowd in the evenings. El Cuartito is not air-conditioned and does not fill with fashionable Argentines, but does serve a mighty pizza.

For lunchtime carnivores, El Desnivel in San Telmo and Lo de Jesus in Palermo Viejo – also open in the evening – are two of the finest steak houses in the city. If you are in the Micro Centro during the day, El Claustro Santa Catalina is a great spot to escape the heat and the traffic.

Angelina, Charcas 3386, Ciudad de Buenos Aires
Tel: 4825 1111
Open: daily, 8.30am until they decide to close

Having just walked out of the Alto Palermo shopping mall with three pairs
of stilettos and two pairs of bottom-hugging Rapsodia jeans – delighted, as
you are, to have squeezed into them, as Argentine girls seem to do with
ease – you need a bite to eat. A 6-minute walk away is Angelina, which,
despite its low profile, serves some of the best ravioli in town. Popular with

a mix of *porteños* and relaxed professionals, Angelina is set on the quiet, ver-
dant end of Charcas street where few tourists tread, its tables spilling out
onto the pavement. The specials here are 'lamb ragú demiglace with carrot
and thyme *ñoquis*' along with the ubiquitous steak sandwich, but the mush-
room-stuffed ravioli never fail to deliver. Angelina gradually fills and refills
throughout the day and is a haven for the heavy-laden.

Bar 6, Armenia 1676, Palermo Viejo
Tel: 4833 6807
Open: 8am until late. Closed Sundays.

A burned-out American trader named Phil who lived in Palermo Viejo went
to Bar 6 for breakfast every day for six months. He loved to slouch down
on the velvet sofas and look up at the tall, cement ceiling and brick walls
while pondering the latest Argentine economic crash over his Clarín newspaper. He would then chat to his favourite waitress, Ines, who he was convinced had fallen in love with him. After enjoying a cup of coffee, a *media*

luna (croissant), yogurt and a glass of orange juice, he would tip Ines well and head home to contemplate lunch, a happy man. The beautiful Ines, smiling inwardly, always looked forward to his next visit. Bar 6 is always an ideal spot for breakfast, tea and cakes, a post-shopping gin and tonic – or for relaxing and

falling in love. It's situated right in the front row of Palermo Viejo's fashion show, so dress to kill – especially at the weekends when local DJs work their chilled beats.

Bengal, Arenales 837, Retiro
Tel: 4314 2926
Open: noon–4pm, 8pm–1am Mon–Fri; 7.30pm–1am Sat. Closed Sundays.

Argentines are terrified of spicy food. Absolutely petrified, in fact. Two twists of the peppermill will have them sweating. As well as its slickly delivered Italian dishes and melt-in-your-mouth *ceviche*, Bengal is famous for its curry. Although not quite Brick Lane standard, these red-hot curries do just fine, given the lack of alternatives in the salted-beef-eating capital of the world.

Bengal, located just off Plaza San Martin, is perfect for a serious business lunch or a carb-load after visiting the English tower opposite the Malvinas (Falklands) War Memorial. This is a serious restaurant, rated highly among local chefs and food lovers, so flip-flops are unadvisable

unless you want to be sniffed at by the stiff Brazilian and Argentine collars next door. Powerful politicians like to eat in the Loi Suites hotel a few yards up the road, where Bengal has a second, hidden branch. Curry-lovers should also note Sottovoce (Av del Libertador 1098, tel: 4807 6691) also serves a mild chicken curry.

La Biela, Quintana, Av. 596, Recoleta
Tel: 4804 0449
Open: daily, 7am (8am Sun)–3am (4am Fri–Sat)

Recoleta's cemetery is one of the city's must-see sights, as is the weekend hippie market offering everything from peace pipes and palm readings to orange juice. Both are just yards away from La Biela, a Buenos Aires high-society classic featuring enormous rubber trees and, oddly, two London-style red telephone boxes. Ironically, you now pay upwards of 25 pesos for a sandwich in a place named after a car's broken connecting rod. Racing drivers Jorge Malbran and Ernesto Tornquist christened this place in the 1950s

after their car ground to a halt on this corner. Now inundated with tourists, who nestle down for an early morning espresso or a late afternoon tipple, La Biela is one of Buenos Aires' ever-green pastures. The elderly waiters are monstrously efficient given the size of the patio, and will always recommend the *sandwich de bife de lomo* (steak sandwich). Do not be tempted to go anywhere else but here (or perhaps Munich - Roberto M. Ortiz 1871, tel: 4804 3981) to eat on the Recoleta strip that continues two blocks to Vicente Lopez.

Cabaña Las Lilas, Alicia Moreau de Justo 516, Puerto Madero
Tel: 4313 1336 www.laslilas.com.ar
Open: daily, noon–3.30pm, 7.30–midnight

Billions of dollars have been poured into Puerto Madero. Miami Beach-type towers are springing up around the docks to form a new high-rise hub in the city. Whether this building site is ultimately destined to be a ghost town is, for the moment, irrelevant. What is not, however, is that this is where you

will find Cabaña Las Lilas, one of Buenos Aires' finest steak houses, and a destination where the better hotel concierges will send their guests to dine in the evening. However, the reality is that no *porteño* with fashion sense will battle through traffic to eat in Puerto Madero during the evening. In addition, few *porteños* are prepared to pay the extortionate prices here, and are deterred by the problem of parking. So come in the day, and admire Puerto Madero's docks and mammoth constructions from Cabaña Las Lilas' terrace. The beef here is exceptional, as is the service. If you do come in the evening, follow dinner with drinks at Buda Bar (see Drink). On Wednesdays even the trendy *porteño* is prepared to take a taxi to party at Puerto Madero's Asia de Cuba.

Chez Pauline, Juncal 1695, Recoleta
Tel: 4816 9988 www.chezpauline.com.ar
Open: 9am (9.30am Sat)–8pm. Closed Sundays.

Given the lack of salad in BA, it's surprising what a simple piece of lettuce can do for you when it's drizzled with real French dressing made by French

121

owner Pauline Rosaz. And if it's tea you're after, Pauline makes delicious cakes and has shipped in over 100 varieties of tea – including delicacies such

as 'Oh La La' and 'Madame Butterfly', as well as the traditional English Breakfast and Earl Grey. Chequered floors and a solid wooden counter await customers, who comprise an eclectic mix of elderly ladies on their way to visit their psychoanalysts, and 20-something local girls with their love interests in tow, who refuse to risk their reputations on dinner dates but are willing to risk an outing in daylight hours. Pauline Rosaz came to Buenos Aires to live quietly, but luckily for the Recoleta neighbourhood she has imported a little Gallic charm, and reminded locals that many of the buildings they live in are, in fact, very French.

El Claustro Santa Catalina, San Martín 705, Micro Centro

Tel: 4312 0235 www.elclaustrosc.com.ar
Open: daily, 12.30–4pm

Why you would want to be in Buenos Aires' Micro Centro during a hot day is anybody's guess. But if you disobeyed our shopping advice and walked down Florida Street as many concierges will advise you, then El Claustro Santa Catalina is your 'little slice of peace' in the city's bustling undergrowth. El Claustro (the cloister) was built in 1745 and was the home to the Santa Catalina nuns who spent their lives knitting, praying and studying within the confines of Santa Catalina's walls. Fortunately the menu has changed since the veil-and-straw-shoes days. Chef Rolando Benitez Cuella has fortified his menu with exquisite salmon, beef and pasta main courses to go alongside his rabbit, chicken and sardine starters. You can dine in the old refectory, but a table in the courtyard under the palm trees is hard to beat, particularly in

this part of town, when the fumes and breakneck pace of Buenos Aires seem a million miles away.

Croque Madame, Av. Libertador 1902 (Museo de Arte Decorativo), Palermo
Tel: 4806 8639
Open: daily, 8am (10am Sat–Sun)–midnight

To really feel Buenos Aires' pulse, at some point you have to sit beside Libertador Avenue and watch the Formula One-aspiring taxi drivers push their Renaults to the limit as they fly towards downtown. You can do this, in relative safety, at Croque Madame, behind the iron gates of the Museo de Arte Decorativo (Museum of Decorative Arts). Croque Madame is situated

in the gate house of the Museum, which is a 20th-century mansion housing over 4,000 pieces ranging from Roman sculptures to contemporary silver. It is open every day except Monday from 2pm until 7pm. Croque Madame, however, opens much earlier in the day and caters for dinner, too. Either pop into the Museum during the day and come for lunch, or for a little respite after shopping. Fountain-side Croque Madame chicken sandwiches are particularly recommended.

El Cuartito, Talcahuano 937, Recoleta
Tel: 4816 1758/4331
Open: daily, noon–late

Brazilians will tell you Pelé is the greatest footballer of all time, Argentines will dare you not to say Diego Maradona. Most *porteños* say this is the best pizza joint in Buenos Aires, others will tell you their local corner shop serves the best – it's as much of a question of taste as it is about competi-

tion. Not only does El Cuartito serve some of the city's most authentic pizza, but the atmosphere is pure old-school Buenos Aires. The strip-lit, 1930s dining hall is packed with 'Diego' memorabilia, photographs and shirts. El Cuartito ('the little room') has little sense of style, but oozes character. The kitchen staff, who look as if they're on the verge of heat exhaustion, will chat away to customers about anything from pre-colonization history to their favourite cumbia art – Bombón Asesino by Ninel Conde is a good one, in case you need a conversation starter. El Cuartito is constantly friendly and always busy, with customers popping in and out all through the afternoon until the end of the evening, when the gates are finally shut. At weekends it becomes a popular haven for high-society locals whose maids are off duty.

La Cupertina, Cabrera 5296, Palermo Viejo
Tel: 4777 3711
Open: noon–midnight. Closed Sundays and Mondays.

Empanadas are a staple starter in the Argentine diet and are usually followed by the traditional *parilla* (grill). The closest English translation of
empanada is 'pasty'. But the
traditionally thick Cornish pasty
bears no resemblance to the
Argentine *empanada*. The standard issue fillings – beef (either
minced or cut); ham and cheese;
cheese, tomato and basil; onion
and cheese; or a rather poky
Stilton and celery – are surrounded by thin pastry and then
cooked in oil, or more com-
monly oven-baked. La Cupertina
is the picky *porteño's* choice for
an *empanada*. Not too crispy,
not too big, and certainly not

too small. You will have to trek up to Palermo Viejo to find La Cupertina, or
alternatively place a large order over the phone and have it delivered.

El Desnivel, Defensa 855, San Telmo
Tel: 4300 9081
Open: daily, noon–4pm, 7.30pm–1am

Founder of El Desnivel, Hernesto Fontanella, passed away during the economic crisis of 2000 – his legacy is one of Buenos Aires' most famed *parillas*.
Now Hernesto's son Luis helms the till, and endearingly swears: 'There are
little angels looking after us. It's thanks to a miracle we are still afloat. When
other restaurants went under, we stayed alive.' Luis is a modest man. There
is regularly a crowd of 50 or so crammed around El Desnivel's door during
the evenings, waiting to get their teeth into some of the fattest steaks in San
Telmo. Diners come for the service, the packed atmosphere, the baked *provoleta* cheese starters, the man-sized steaks and the flan with *dulce de leche*.
To avoid the crowds, come during the day and enjoy the patio at the rear.

'*Desnivel*' means 'uneven', a reference to the grubby interior, which is a far cry from the food. Turn up for lunch. Luis will give you a hug, and you will toddle off to San Telmo more than satisfied.

Florencio, Francisco de Vitoria 2363, Recoleta
Tel: 4807 6477
Open: 8am–8pm. Closed Sundays.

When it comes to sweet little cafés, hidden in the back streets of arguably the smartest neighbourhood in the city, Florencio could not climb any higher. Recoleta's 'Isla' is built north of Puyreddon avenue, a 5-minute walk from the Recoleta cemetery on raised ground – hence the term 'island' – over-

looking the Evita monuments and the city's national library with its arborescent architecture. The library will confuse you at first glance, but Florencio's teatime rogels – an Argentine *dulce de leche* speciality – or chocolate devils are as honest as they come, and as delicious as they are fattening. Florencio is also supposedly just around the corner from the Buenos Aires home of pop star Shakira. The diminutive café has a capacity of around 10, which means Nicolas the waiter treats customers as though they are 'en casa'. English china, English tea, delicious cakes and a warm Anglo–Argentine atmosphere await customers. Early dinners are also served.

Gioia, Palacio Duhau Park Hyatt, Avenida Alvear 1661, Recoleta

Tel: 5171 1234 www.buenosaires.park.hyatt.com
Open: daily, 8am–midnight

If you like polo, this place is ideal for a snack before heading up town to watch the Argentine Open in December – you might well cross paths with

Patrick Hermès, as in 'Hermès of Paris' fame, who stays here before he takes his official seat at Palermo (see Play, page 197). Lunch at Gioia is rather like dining with royalty. The surroundings – the Palacio Duhau, a 20th-century mansion – are indeed palatial, you'll get the best Italian buffet in the city, and it all seems to go rather well with a bottle of chilled chardonnay. The Park Hyatt clientele are a wealthy (albeit not necessarily sophisticated) crowd. Booking a table at one of the raised decks beside the ornamental lap pool is imperative if you are to max the experience, and as far as the food goes, the steamed salmon with beetroot and the ravioli take some beating. Sunday brunch is arguably superior to the Alvear Palace Hotel or the Four Seasons, but if you're staying here you may feel obliged to try another luncheon spot.

I Fresh Market, Azucena Villaflor, Blvd. y Cossenttini, Puerto Madero

Tel: 5775 0330 www.ifreshmarket.com.ar
Open: 8am–midnight daily

Life is too short not to live it intensely – that is I Fresh Market's motto (and come to think of it, ours as well), which may seem a slight contradiction since this is an organic-food-shop-cum-restaurant priding itself on healthy living. Worry not. Organic food has not yet kicked off in Buenos Aires, but at I Fresh Market, you will find delicious alternatives to the toasted ham and

cheese *tostados* the Argentines seem to live on, as well as a wide selection of salads and vegetable tarts. Try one of Borja Blázquez's hot pastrami and pickle sandwiches. Doesn't sound very organic? Well, no. But we are told it's healthy if

prepared correctly. It may be a bit of a trek to find (all the way down to Puerto Madero) but it's worth it, and if you are staying at the Faena Hotel (see Sleep), this is ideally placed for you. I Fresh Market is subtly lit and works for a quirkier out-of-the-way dinner date, before you head off to Buda Bar and then Asia de Cuba on a Wednesday evening.

Krishna, Malabia 1833, Palermo Viejo

Tel: 4833 4618
Open: noon–midnight Tues–Sun. Closed Mondays and Tuesday evenings.

Luckily, lunch at Krishna is not all about self-realization, God-realization, Bhakti-yoga and spiritual life. Rather it is about *'comida rica, sana, que tiene pocas calorias'* – tasty, healthy food that keeps the waistline trim – as *porteñas* say with a smile. In Buenos Aires, the females of the species look thin, pretty and sculpted because they take care to look after themselves. Krishna serves tasty vegetarian Indian food that is, well, very healthy. So it

figures at lunchtime, dozens of the young and attractive congregate here. If you can handle a plate of spiced soya meat, then you could meet the lithe, holistic yoga instructor of your dreams. Krishna does its meditating in front of Plaza Palermo Viejo, around which hundreds of boutique shops are popping up in the cobbled backstreets.

Lima Limo, Canal Este, Delta del Tigre
Open: daily, noon–close

What on earth a yellow ski igloo straight from the Andes is doing riverside on the Tigre delta is anyone's guess. But it's here and it now hovers above the flood plains, along with two further wooden decks and walkways. Either drive down to the river – which takes 25 minutes with an attacking driver at the wheel – and take a wakeboarding trip up the river to find Lima Limo, or hop into a helicopter (see Play), which will land you on the doorstep. The

Delta from above is spectacular. At weekends Lima Limo becomes crammed with *porteños* who own riverside retreats, but during the week it remains a quietly beautiful spot for lunch. Tie up your speed boat or glide in on your landing craft for ravioli (large enough to satisfy an army of Italian soldiers), or pizza and beef that would meet the approval of even the pickiest *porteño*. Intoxicated somersaults off the pier are encouraged.

Lo de Jesus, Gurruchaga 1406 esq. Cabrera, Palermo Viejo
Tel: 4831 1961 www.lodejesus.com.ar
Open: daily, noon–4pm, 7.30pm–closing

Lo de Jesus was here before Palermo Viejo went crazy with boutique shops and stylish restaurants. Owner 81-year-old Jesus Pernas started out in 1953 selling vegetables and the odd plateful of beef; now Lo de Jesus is a Palermo Viejo classic that boasts a loyal crowd of fashionable regulars – including the author who used to live 30 metres away – while still staying close to its

roots. Thoroughly Argentine, and quaintly decorated with original chequer-board flooring, dark panelling and mirrors for the ladies and Buenos Aires' increasingly effeminate men, Lo de Jesus buzzes in the day and flutters its eyelashes a little more in the evening. We recommend you face Lo de Jesus head on and order one of chef Ariel Soares de Almeida's *bife de chorizos* with an egg on top. Salads, cold cuts and fish are also available if you fancy something more refined. Book ahead for an evening table, otherwise you can chew the fat until 4pm during the day.

Lobby, Nicaragua 5944 Palermo Hollywood
Tel: 4770 9335
Open: daily, 9am–1am

A bunch of Buenos Aires' budding sommeliers and established barmen take pride in taking it extremely easy at Lobby. Join them for a glass of malbec before trotting off for dinner at Green Bamboo, Sudestada or Standard. Opened in 2006, this is supposed to be a wine bar, and the wall full of bottles means Lobby is dressed like one, but its highly unpretentious atmosphere in the back streets of Palermo Viejo is somewhat refreshing. Simply

raise your eyebrows and a waiter will be on hand to fill your glass. Either head outside and relax beside the cobbled street, head upstairs to the colossal sofas, or perch on a white leather chair in the restaurant. Oui Oui is just up the road for a French snack, while lunch here is a good choice.

Mark's Deli, El Salvador 4701, Palermo Viejo
Tel: 4832 6244   www.marks.com.ar
Open: 8.30am–9.30pm Mon–Sat; 10.30am–9pm Sundays and holidays

Your table at Mark's is perched right in the heart of the Palermo Soho revolution. This corner café is hard to beat as a place to stop off, dump your shopping bags and crunch the ice of your homemade lemonade. According to the fashionistas, Mark's serve the best sandwiches in the city; in reality, they're not quite as good as they used to be – the sandwich stuffers have moved on from when Mark's became really cool, back in 2003. A hip, albeit touristy hang-out, along with I Fresh Market, Mark's offers an alternative to the classic Buenos Aires ham and cheese *tostada* – which has led to the

Argentine press slating Mark's menu as being too American. Bearing the Miami/New York stamp of maximum minimalism, the setting is stark but comfortable: an informal lounge with efficient waitresses and tasty orange plastic stools, which match the building's mandarin awnings.

In terms of clientele, you'll be hard-pressed to find a more committed bunch of shopaholics.

Museo de Evita, J.M. Gutierrez 3926, Palermo
Tel: 4800 1599
Open: 9am until they decide to close. Closed Mondays.

Restaurant Museo de Evita epitomizes the saying '*buena onda*' – 'good karma'. This quirky little garden restaurant is situated on a quiet street in Palermo's posh residential neighbourhood. Friendly waiters serve chef

Daniel Cid's Argentine–Italian dishes, such as risotto with osso buco, scalloped beef, a selection of pastas and the traditional Argentine chunk of beef with rustic mashed potato. Customers start to arrive for a late breakfast, then begin to drip in for lunch. It's an all-day kind of place that knowledge-able locals take pride in because it's slightly off the beaten track, and it incorporates a touch of history: the real Evita Museum is just around the corner at Lafinur 2988. The museum was opened on 26 July 2002 to mark the 50th anniversary of Eva Peron's death, and exhibits all kinds of memora-bilia from the 1950s including her clothing. Get your teeth into a bit of Argentine culture and then pile into Daniel's carb-loading mashed potato.

El Obrero, Agustín Caffarena 64 (between Ministro Brin and Caboto), La Boca
Tel: 4362 9912
Open: noon–4pm, 8pm–closing. Closed Sundays.

As your taxi pulls off the road onto a dirt track, heads under the motorway and eventually stops beside a down-and-out building, you'll be questioning whether this is the same Obrero everyone's told you about before you set off to La Boca. Don't be worried, this is the normal approach to the area's most famous culinary son. Inside Obrero, the walls are cluttered with foot-ball scarves, soda bottles, more football memorabilia, a few more Boca Juniors crests and, of course, pictures of 'El Diego' lifting the Jules Rimet in 1986. Like El Desnivel in San Telmo, the walls appear to be crumbling down around you, and *los baños* resemble an out-house. But the indoor grill, whose chimney pokes out of the interior walls, is idolized for its *bife de*

chorizo (steak). You are here for a classic Argentine meat feast, so loosen your belt and take your time.

Oui Oui, Nicaragua 6068, Palermo Hollywood
Tel: 4778 9614
Open: 8am–8pm Tue–Fri; 8am to 10am – 8pm Sat–Sun

Ladies, this one's for you: lovely candles, sweet cakes, scented tables and pink upholstery, trashy magazines to read, really, really soft napkins, the occasional cute French love song playing in the background and just the friendliest staff in the world. Boys are welcome, but play by girls' rules here

– you'll be given a scented napkin with your stuffed crois-sant or cake whether you like it or not. Okay, that's a slight exaggera-tion; but Rocio Garcia Orza's Oui Oui has developed a fine following of young ladies and the lunchtime nattering goes on all afternoon. There is no booking a table here. If full, try the Lobby wine bar (see Snack), located a block away, which is also excellent for lunch.

Pizza Cero, Tagle 2661, Palermo Viejo
Tel: 4803 3449   www.pizzacero.com.ar
Open: 7am–3am Mon–Wed; 24 hours Thurs–Sun.

Forget the pizza and forget the other branches of this pizzeria chain you may see in Puerto Madero or in San Isidro. This one has a lot more going for it – and not least, the incredible opening hours. It's popular with a highly attractive young Argentine crowd, who pop in for an early beer and a bite, or for one of the fabulous ice-creams, on their way back from an after-noon's shopping in Palermo Viejo. If you are feeling confident about moving to Buenos Aires permanently, this Pizza Cero also doubles up as a Mini showroom. The owner believes they are ideal for weaving through Buenos Aires' traffic at pace. Intriguingly, Pizza Cero also sports a wine-mixing bar, the idea being that you can blend your Malbec with your Cabernet

Sauvignon, Syrah or Merlot. A relaxing, if alcoholic, way to end an afternoon's shopping and warm up for the evening.

Providencia, Golpee Fuerte, Cabrera 5995, Palermo Hollywood
Tel: 4772 8507
Open: 11am–4pm. Closed Saturdays and Sundays.

Some Argentines have begun to slate underground, 'secret' restaurants, but those who know their food and enjoy the arty atmosphere (think moustached Mexican artist wearing a flowery shirt), love to lunch here. Bang (hard) on the door and gain entry to the pasta, bread and jam factory, which has no sign, simply an orange sheet of paper saying *'Golpee Fuerte'*. In fact, nobody is really sure what this place is called. Upstairs is what resembles an old mechanic's warehouse where artists sketch away – overlooking the

kitchen – while downstairs the *madres* work on their pasta, bread and jam. Take a seat at a long communal wooden table in the centre of the kitchen, watch the sunlight poke through the corrugated iron door beside the rack of freshly baked bread, and order a jug of homemade lemonade and a delicious bowl of pasta sautéed with mixed herbs, eggs, vegetables, oil and cheese. Hygiene laws were invented because places like this exist, but have faith: those who make the pasta are the ones who cook it, and they do so with passion and flair.

Voulez Bar, Cerviño 3802, Palermo Chico
Tel: 4802 4817
Open: daily, 8am–midnight (12.30am Fri–Sat)

Get your teeth into Palermo Chico's residential neighbourhood. Corner café Voulez Bar has a dedicated following of wealthy girls who still live with their parents, budding professionals still junior enough to get away from the offices during the day, and their bosses on a break. This is a real locals' place – to come and drink coffee, criticize people's outfits, gaze at svelte

Argentine figures and talk about whose house they are going to stay at in Punta del Este during the summer. The chunky diced lamb sandwiches are to be shared, unlike the cakes, which girls seem to guard with their lives. The coffee is served in French china, not the usual Italian brand espresso cups, and the chat, generally, is very enjoyable to overhear ('She shouldn't be eating that. Do you know how many complex carbs there are in an angel cake?'). Voulez Bar is for breakfast, late breakfast, brunch, lunch, tea and dinner – whatever vous voulez.

Yacht Club Argentino, Viamonte y Río de la Plata, Dársena Norte, Puerto Madero
Tel: 4311 4648 www.yca.org.ar
Open: daily, noon–3.30pm

Perched at the end of Puerto Madero with the River Plate lapping at its feet, this is the only yacht club to speak of in Capital Federal and is a great spot for lunch on a sunny day. To enter you must be affiliated with another yacht club – any will do. But if you just call ahead and mention a yacht club (even if you're not strictly a member of one), there should be no problem in getting past security. There are times in Buenos Aires when a little white lie

is worth telling. The club was formed in 1883, but the clubhouse was built in 1915. Sailing veterans such as Chay Blythe – who completed the first westward circumnavigation of the world – to mention one, have told their tales of icebergs and 50-foot waves here. This is the heartbeat of yachting in central Buenos Aires; procure a table under the tree beside the clubhouse for a unique view of the river.

party...

Clubbing in Buenos Aires is an art form. While most foreigners are understandably intimidated by the steely glares of the *porteñas*, what lies behind the pouting faces are some of the most friendly, outgoing clubbers in the southern hemisphere. Argentines can be a sceptical bunch at first, but when they realize you are a respectful, hands-off clubber, there to hear some of the world's top DJs work their magic, they will make you want to stay and party in Buenos Aires forever.

The party scene in Buenos Aires caters for all tastes and energy levels, so when the birds start singing at around 5am, rest assured there is a nightclub beginning to warm up – one that will stay hot until it's either time for Argentines to saddle up for work, or time for the after-party locations to open their gates to Buenos Aires' hungry-for-more nocturnal warriors. Technically, you can party all day and all night in Buenos Aires, but you have to know where, at what time and what night to turn up.

Following the 2004 nightclub disaster, when 190 were killed in a fire, President Kirshner's government cracked down on what was an almost unrestricted free-for-all. Now, once heaving weekend venues have been forced to close their doors. What's left are the old-timers, the clubs that made Buenos Aires famous for its raves (Pacha and Mint, for example), new clubs who have remodelled old venues (Crobar) and a few fresh faces created to suit the latest laws (Jet and Sunset).

The consequences are that Buenos Aires' nightlife is now easier to navigate and less hit-and-miss than before. Asia de Cuba, Crobar, Mint, Pacha and Rumi are the best places in Buenos Aires for trance, house and techno. For more of a lounge setting in Palermo Viejo, Podesta is open at weekends, the reopened Jet on the Costanera suits the less energetic but in-vogue clubber, while Ink provides more of a footballers' wives, champagne-on-ice setting.

As always, the key is to know who will be partying where on any given night.

On a Wednesday night: Asia de Cuba in Puerto Madero and Belgrano-based Rumi lead the way where Tequila (once BA's most exclusive club) left off, drawing in an exclusive, indecently attractive crowd. Bahrein and Museum follow at a distance.

On Thursday night you will discover Buenos Aires' alternative *punchi-punchi* beats and find hip-hop at Araoz, while Maluco Beleza, the wildcard in the pack, will teach you a thing or two about Brazilian dancing. Other good choices are Niceto Club and, Club 69's new host, Roxy.

During the weekend: at Pacha you are guaranteed to bump into the pilled-up-to-the-eyeballs clubber; at Crobar you'll find the best looking, coolly controlled dance fanatic driven purely by the house beats; while at Mint there'll be a mixture of both. From Pacha and Mint, clubbers can watch the sun come up over the river before they head to the after-party clubs on Sunday morning.

In general, nightclubs in Buenos Aires are predominantly either found in the Centre or on the Costanera (on the shores of the River Plate near the city's airport), only 15 minutes by taxi from Recoleta or Palermo.

Getting into a nightclub in Buenos Aires can be tricky if you turn up at peak hours, so take note of the club promoters we mention for particular club, and mention that Hg2 sent you. Otherwise, it's the usual story – the best looking, the best-dressed and the most confident types who avoid the queue. Entrance costs AR$15–30 for men and no more than AR$15 for women. Alternatively, book a table to guarantee entry.

For those tortured by Argentine *histericismo* ('mind games'), Buenos Aires' adult entertainment is full-on. The term 'sex sells' is to be taken literally in Buenos Aires, and we have selected the best of the city's above-board establishments, including Diego Maradona's favourite.

Araoz, Araoz 2424, Palermo

Tel: 4833 7775

Open: 1–7am Thurs, Fri and Sat

Hip-hop is a growing force in Buenos Aires, becoming a real alternative to the electronic house beats that echo out over the River Plate. You come to Araoz for the *Thursday Lost Party*, which throbs with an eclectic Buenos Aires crowd of wannabe Big Daddy Kanes, stunning *porteñas* in tight, revealing outfits, and those who simply fancy a night off from the trendy, house music lounges. Although its Palermo location is inconspicuous, Araoz has

won a dedicated following since 2004, with the regulars coming back every night for more. Don't spoil a good thing; stick to Thursday night's dunk and slam parties, and try not to dress like a gangster unless you really believe you can pull it off.

Asia de Cuba, Pierina Dialessi 750, Puerto Madero

Tel: 4894 1328   www.asiadecuba.com.ar

Open: 9pm–5am. Closed Sundays and Mondays.

When Tequila closed, Asia de Cuba picked up the crowd and added them to an already glitzy fan base. Like Rumi, the restaurant transforms into a nightclub after dinner, but bear in mind the cold ravioli, sushi and steak on offer here are secondary to the feast of A-list models (both boys and girls) for the eyes. Asia de Cuba's ethos is, by definition, a Latin/Asian-inspired fusion, which the interior décor religiously adheres to, although as the night wears on, provenance is long forgotten. The crowd is a ridiculously attractive and

affluent bunch of *porteños* and open-mouthed tourists, who have never seen anything so incredible in their lives. The VIP section is reserved for models, local heroes and those in the loop. To secure entry via the club's guest list contact Moi Altuna (www.moialtuna.com).

Bahrein, Alsina 940, Centre
Tel: 4331 3231   www.bahreinba.com
Open: from 12.30am Tues, Wed, Fri and Sat

Originally a bank, formerly a strip club and now a nightclub, the Downtown-based Bahrein, which opened in 2004, perfectly fills the Tuesday night hiatus in Buenos Aires' after-hours social schedule with the 160 drum'n'bass night, led by resident DJ Bad Boy Orange. Through the blackout curtains and past the vintage chandelier, the ground floor is a chic, white-leather sofa, chill-out lounge, while the basement, where the bank vault VIP area is housed, is Bahrein's trademark. If you're lucky, this is where you'll end up ordering

your fifth drink of the evening, having had dinner at Juana M, cocktails at Dadá or Milión, followed by drinks at La Cigale before strolling in here for a few more. Bahrein is a good mid-week club, particularly for that elusive Tuesday night party.

Le Click, Rivadavia 1910, Centre
Tel: 4543 4183
Open: midnight–7am Fri–Sat

A wildcard in le pack, Le Click, formerly La Antigua nightclub, has a dark, subterranean vibe to it. On Friday and Saturday nights the gay-friendly crowd enjoys the session with resident DJ, Romina Cohn. This cavernous venue is packed with up to a thousand clubbers, most of whom revel in Le Click's air of urban grit. An unpretentious, alternative scene means the club-bers are generally very approachable. The events here do vary, so have your

concierge call ahead to see whether the night you are planning to attend is actually what you had in mind. Le Click is the kind of club you visit if you are in Buenos Aires for more than a week, but proba-bly worth passing on if you are only in town for a couple of days. It's an edgy, underground club that thumps out the beats well into the morning.

Crobar, Paseo de La Infanta, Avenida del Libertador 3883, Palermo
Tel: 4778 1500 www.crobar.com.ar
Open: 10pm–6am Fri–Sat

Formerly Buenos Aires News, Crobar is now the city's leading club and, as the new addition to the empire, has cheekily outdone its Crobar cousins in Chicago, New York and Miami. Top DJs, hardly any drugs, the most beautiful people in BA and a VIP section that looks straight over the main dance-floor are all crowd-pullers here. Crobar is one of those clubs you want to truly absorb into your senses, so feel free roam the bars: the view is spectacular

from every angle and each bar has its own set of people. With the recent addition of El Punto, a rock music hall, to the end of the main dance-floor, Crobar has become what can only be described as a superclub that's here to stay. Contact Moi Altuna (www.moialtuna.com) if you want to skip the queues.

Cuernavaca, Bolívar 518, Pilar
Tel: 15 4447 2428 www.cuernavaca.com.ar
Open: from 11pm Fri–Sat

If you're an aspiring polo player, then this one's for you. Cuernavaca is Pilar's local 'Mediterranean' nightclub where the resident DJ plays what he calls

una ensalada mixta ('a mixed salad') of everything, where the Eye of the Tiger, YMCA, Madonna, Cumbia Villera, commercial trance and the Rolling Stones are all tossed up. Dressing the salad is a following of 20-somethings who have popped out from their weekend houses after the family barbecue, the polo crowd who keep their stable of ponies in Pilar Chico and a sprinkling of the older generation out for a dance with the missus. This is a lightweight alternative to the Buenos Aires clubbing scene, with a hassle-free vibe and a friendly atmosphere. You do, however, have to drive for an hour from the centre of BA to get here.

Ink, Niceto Vega 5635, Palermo Hollywood
Tel: 4777 6242
Open: from 10pm Fri–Sun

Ink attracts a fascinating mixture of football players and their entourages, as well as a lorry-load of silicone-enhanced blondes. It hovers slightly below

the radar of Buenos Aires' more elite clubbers, who shun Ink as being '*grasa*' (tacky). Pay no attention to them. Ink can play a key role in the warm-up to a colossal night in Buenos Aires. Pop in for a drink and a dance at 1am on a Friday or Saturday night before moving on at 2am. Aesthetically this is almost as hi-tech as it gets in Buenos Aires, and the tried and tested progressive trance beats, in sync with the giant screens above the dance-floor, get the heart pumping and will put you in the mood for a less plastic but more explosive nightclub.

Jet, Avenida Rafael Obligado 4801, Costanera Norte
Tel: no telephone
Open: from 12.30pm Fri–Sat

Illuminated in neon, small enough to be a bar, but large enough to be a nightclub, Jet is Buenos Aires' version of a Miami lounge. Grab a beer from the Battlestar Galactica-style bar and ask the chiselled male and svelte female models how to behave. Some words of advice might be to look as if nothing phases you, strut around wiggling your bottom and dance like you are the king of the world, for you are the king of the world at Jet, and this is

your dance-floor. We also recommend you don't listen to a word they say. For some Argentines, going out dancing is more about being seen than actually having fun, so order another drink at the bar, sit down at one of the sofa booths overlooking the dance-floor and pick the best anthem for showing off your moves.

Maluco Beleza, Sarmiento 1728, Centre
Tel: 4372 1737 www.malucobeleza.com.ar
Open: from 10pm Wed, Fri–Sun

The Brazilian prostitutes who turn up here regularly are not the reason why Maluco Beleza fills on a Sunday night. You come here on a Sunday night because first of all, there are few other clubs open on a Sunday; second, dancing to Brazilian music with Brazilians is hugely entertaining; and, third, when else are you going to get to one of Buenos Aires' Cumbia nightclubs? Maluco Beleza is therefore one of the only safe places to sample some real

145

Latin dance music with real Latinos. Maluco Beleza fills with semi-professional dancers, those keen to try something different and tourists curious to meet Brazilian hookers.

Mint, Avenida Costanera Rafael Obligado and Costanera Norte

Tel: 4806 8002 www.mint-argentina.com.ar
Open: from 1.20am Fri–Sat. Closed during January.

Mint has the middle ground in Buenos Aires. Heavier than Crobar, not as druggy as Pacha, this is the happy medium between insane club land and fashionable hysteria. Mint's main dance-floor is surrounded by VIP lounges, with a smaller hip-hop room and an al-fresco chill-out space for watching the sun rise over the Plate. To really pimp yourself, book a table above the main dance-floor or in the VIP section behind the DJ. For mortals, the main

dance-floor, on which the usual attractive band of *porteños* mixes with wide-eyed tourists, is quite sufficient. Both Friday and Saturday nights attract an up-for-it crowd, but if pressed we would visit Crobar on a Friday, Mint on Saturday and Caix on Sunday morning. Nothing smarter than a T-shirt and jeans will do.

Museum, Peru 535, San Telmo
Tel: 4771 9628
Open: from 6pm Wed

After-office parties at Museum on Wednesday evenings heave, as you would expect, with suited and booted Argentines up for an après board-meeting rampage. It's essentially a rectangular cell-block with three storeys of balconies, each overlooking the main dance-floor from all angles, and crammed with office workers. Each of the balconies has a different sponsor and a different bar, but all convey the same message: get drunk with fellow workers, and then go home and sleep it off. Why would you go to an after-office party if you haven't been working? Argentines love letting their hair down,

are always in the mood to party and enjoy practising their English on foreigners. However, be prepared to be squashed in for a long wait at the bar. We recommend you head to the Marlboro-sponsored first-floor balcony, grab a table and order drinks from the waitress. The food here is poor to average, but then few chefs could pull off gourmet perfection for 2,000 hungry secretaries and their love interests.

Niceto, Niceto Vega 5510, Palermo Hollywood
Tel: 4779 9396 www.nicetoclub.com
Open: from 12.30am Thurs–Fri, 1am Sat

Thursday's Club 69 at Niceto was the stuff of legends for its transvestite shows and general debauchery, while regular live music events boost Niceto's reputation as a finger-on-the-pulse club. With a main dance-floor overlooked by a stage, a VIP section surveying both, and a smaller bar hidden at the back, Niceto is one of the darkest tunnels in the city, but will continue to draw the crowds with the eclectic events it puts on. Niceto is a destination club for an event, rather than a spur-of-the-moment chic watering-hole. It's a charmingly gritty venue in the scruffy part of Palermo Hollywood, and in-the-know locals – who don't seem to  have a day job – come here for the live music programme.

Palacio Alsina, Adolfo Alsina 940, Centre
Tel: 4331 1277 www.palaciobuenosaires.com
Open: from 1.30am Fri–Sat

If a thousand or so sweaty male clubbers, clad in wife-beaters, crammed into what feels like an old cathedral, tempts you, then Palacio is the crown jewel of all nightclubs on a Sunday night. This is when Palacio hosts the Gay Party, the largest in Buenos Aires' growing gay scene. On Saturday nights, however, the venue hosts Big One – alongside Pacha's Clubland, the city's most serious electronic club night. It goes without saying that most of the crowd will be under some form of chemical anesthesia. If the main dance-floor becomes too hectic, retreat to the first-floor chill-out room, gaze down on the Boschian mayhem below and reflect on Buenos Aires' undying thirst for trance beats, pills and cat tranquillizers. The city's club scene has developed over the years but club kids on pills is still the order of the day over here. Alsina hosts a range of top name international and domestic talent playing genre crossing electroncia. Palacio Alsina is not our favourite club by any means, but the Sunday night sweat fest is as vibrant as it gets for the gay community in BA.

Pacha, Avenida Costanera Rafael Obligado y La Pampa, Costanera Norte
Tel: 4788 4280 www.pachabuenosaires.com
Open: from midnight Fri, and 2am Sat

It's a cliché, but watch the sun come up as others come up around you. Turn up at three, stumble out at eight and move on to Caix for the after-party. If you want clubbing, then this is Buenos Aires' Ibiza, and it's not for the faint-hearted or for those without sunglasses. An extraordinarily dedicated, drugged-up-to-the-eyeballs horde of house, trance and hard-beat fanatics dance through the weekend as if their lives depended on it – although Pacha

also attracts the odd music aficionado there simply to enjoy the beats without artificial stimulation. It's best to spend the extra money and get yourself in the VIP section (email vip@pachabuenosaires.com). Many big-name European DJs have spun here, but look out for Argentines Hernán Catáneo and Carlos Alfonsín, who never fail to take a room to a state of delirium.

Podesta, Armenia 1740, Palermo Viejo
Tel: 4832 2776 www.elpodesta.com.ar
Open: from 11pm Thurs–Sat

This is the only nightclub you want to visit in the heart of Palermo Viejo. Appealing to lounge lovers, the two floors play a mix of cheesy rock and

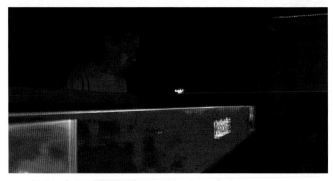

pop classics, along with more hectic trance beats. Podesta attracts a more grounded crowd: attractive, wealthy enough to pay for overpriced energy drinks and secure in the knowledge they can have a good time without the presence of Buenos Aires' glitterati. The two floors are littered with tables (which you can reserve) and the big screen downstairs illuminates an otherwise dark affair, where the lounge-lizards clamber onto the tables and sofas for a dance. Podesta is ideal for an hour's warm up before heading on to a more serious club, such as Mint or Crobar, or alternatively start downstairs and finish off the evening with a techno shake up.

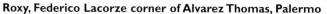

Roxy, Federico Lacorze corner of Alvarez Thomas, Palermo

www.theroxybsas.com.ar

Open: from midnight Thurs–Sat

With the exception of Thursday night's Club 69 and its transvestite shows, eclectic crowd and hard house sets, which has been appropriated from Niceto, Roxy is all about being cheesy. Frequented by students with a love of rock music and Cumbia classics, such as Bombón Asesino, Roxy provides

the weekday clubber with a beer-fuelled, head-banging session (yes, remember, these are students). As the DJ flips on Guns 'n' Roses, the youngish girls dance into tighter protective circles, and the pack of young Argentine studs begin the hunt, you might find yourself wondering what planet you're on or what year you're in. Arrive after 2am clutching your ID – irrespective of how many grey hairs you have – and Roxy will give you a pretension-free glimpse of Buenos Aires' youth in their element.

Rumi, Avenida Figueroa Alcorta 6442, Belgrano

Tel: 4782 1307   www.rumiba.com.ar

Open: from 10pm Wed–Sat

Rumi is said to be the most mystical poet in the history of Islam, and every 17 December for the last seven centuries he is remembered by his ancestors and poets. Rumi is also remembered every Wednesday, Friday and Saturday night, by Argentine goddesses – the same crowd as Asia de Cuba – and their pursuers. True to the restaurant/bar full-on-nightclub culture of BA, dinner is served first before the tables are plucked off the dance-floor

and the electronic party is let loose. The drinking, the dancing and the feeling you have arrived in heaven, which should remind you why you came to Buenos Aires, make up for an underwhelming culinary experience. Along with Asia de Cuba, Rumi attracts a more arrogant, trend-setting crowd – so get your game face on and remember that deep down, behind the 'how-dare-you-look-at-me' glares, fashionable Argentines are kind people that just happen to take pleasure in intimidating foreigners. Thursday night is mature couples' date night.

Sunset, Roque Saenz Peña 440, Olivos
Tel: 4794 8585
Open: 10pm–7am Sat

While the president resides in this Olivos neighbourhood, any Argentine with an ounce of fashion sense will tell you that Sunset is the most tacky, cheesy, footballers' wives, after-shave-soaked pit in town. They are right. Sunset is just that, but also provides a glimpse of the real Buenos Aires, and delivers a brilliant, although somewhat alternative night out. The music policy is eclectic to say the

least: the two dance-floors play anything from Cumbia music to trance, while overworked barmen serve mediocre drinks from the bars. Additionally an outdoor patio, swimming pool and two VIP rooms form the remainder of the club. Occasional live music shows and strippers entertain the inebriated revellers when they're bored of self-love. If the cut-throat Buenos Aires scene is getting the better of you, take a break with a night at Sunset, and return home when the sun rises and it's time for the after-party.

AFTER HOURS

Arkos, Avenida Casares, corner of Avenida Sarmiento, Palermo

Tel: 4804 2512 www.clubarkos.com.ar
Open: from 2am Sat, 7am Sun

An after-hours veteran Arkos, with capacity for 1,200, has been revamped and clubbers pour in on Saturday and Sunday mornings for a Sabbath sweat-box session. On a Sunday morning don't even bother turning up before 8am, when you do you'll need to have similarly large pupils as those around you to survive the session. Caix (see below) is all about sunlight, while Arkos is about prolonging the darkness of the night before.

Caix, Avenida Rafael Obligado, Costanera Norte

Tel: 4806 9749 www.caix-ba.com.ar
Open: from 1am Sat, 9am–3pm Sun

Sunglasses and sweatbands are a must. The most famous of the after-hours venues, Caix is also the finest – the slightly 'accelerated' crowd of regulars will vouch for this. It's our choice for a Sunday-morning after-burn until mid-day, and then if you're really still awake it's the perfect time to go wake-boarding in Tigre (see Play). Now that's true hedonism.

La Conzuelo, corner of Cabrera and Humboldt, Palermo Hollywood
Open: 7am–noon Fri

Friday mornings at La Conzuelo after Club 69 (remember that Roxy is the new venue for Club 69) have become popular with the Kim y Novak tranny

crowd (see Drink). The great thing about La Conzuelo is that it's easy to get in and out of if things get too heavy inside. This small corner club is only for the most dedicated of Friday morning clubbers.

Pinar de Rocha, Av. 2° Rivadavia 14751, Ramos Mejía
Tel: 4654 2273   www.pinarderocha.com
Open: 7am–7pm Sun

For the after after-party. Pinar de Rocha takes the after-party concept to the next level by offering a nightclub that continues through Sunday morning, afternoon and evening. After that, why not just go out again? We wish you the very best of luck.

Transformations, Aguero 726, Centre
Open: 5am–2pm Fri–Sun

This has to be the weirdest place in Buenos Aires. Transformations have indeed taken place. Exceptionally deceptive shemales roam this grotty cavern, drag queens perform on stage, and the house music pounds away until the merry men stumble out into the scorching sun. Do not go alone.

TANGO

Bar el Chino, Beazley 3566, Pompeya
Tel: 4911 0215 www.barelchinofilm.com.ar
Open: 10pm–5am Fri–Sat

They call Jorge Eduardo Garcés 'El Chino' – the Chinaman. His bar, El Chino, is to be found in the Pompeya neighbourhood, where tango has its roots. The café is a covered in tango memorabilia, while El Chino himself claims the tango is danced here the way it was 60 years ago. Make time to meet the Chinaman and you'll love watching tango – the old way – at this rustic little bar in the middle of nowhere.

Bar Sur, Estados Unidos 299, San Telmo
Tel: 4362 6086 www.bar-sur.com.ar
Open: daily, 8pm–3am

You can either heed the advice of your concierge, who will send you to a hideously expensive and over-the-top dinner followed by a tango show, or you can go to the intimate Bar Sur, have a little dinner in this quaint San Telmo corner and enjoy a show where the protagonists involve the audience – and everybody in the room has a smile on their face. Bar Sur is a gentle tango baptism.

Café Tortoni, Avenida de Mayo 829, Micro Centro
Tel: 4342 4328 www.cafetortoni.com.ar
Open: 8am–3am Mon–Sat, 9am–1am Sun

Argentina's oldest café, the Tortoni opened in 1858. While this is a tourist
trap all through the day, Argentines who know their tango still come here to
see shows in the little *sala alfonsina* at the back from 10.30pm. The authenticity has been retained and the tango is top of the range.

La Catedral, Sarmiento 4006, Almagro
Tel: 15 5325 1630 clasesdetangoenlacate@hotmail.com
Open: daily, 9pm–5am. Classes on Mondays, Tuesdays and Fridays at 9.30pm.

La Catedral was the most underground tango dancing-spot in Buenos Aires

until 2004, when the tourists began to pour in. It was then closed down due to fire restrictions before opening again in early 2007. This old warehouse space has been turned into a beautifully rustic tango hall, filled with old sofas and chairs and overlooked by a bar that was once the occupant's kitchen. If you fancy trying out the classes, call ahead and ask for Valeria or Federico, depending on your preference. Remember that men used to dance together, so don't be scared to tread the boards with Federico.

La Dama de Bollini, Pasaje Bollini 2281, Barrio Norte
Tel: 4805 6309 www.ladama-debollini.com.ar
Open: daily, from 7pm

'At 8pm on Wednesday night you are coming to dance tango', we were told. By the end of the evening, more than a little progress had been made. Tucked away in Recoleta, La Dama de Bollini is ultra-accessible. There's no need to tramp all the way down to San Telmo to have a dance – simply satisfy your tango whim and head back around the corner to more hedonistic pursuits. Celtic music is played on Friday nights (10pm), jazz is performed on Saturdays (10pm), and there are also literary meetings on Tuesday evenings (7.30pm) – Jorge Luis Borges attended the first ever gathering.

LIVE MUSIC

Bar Seddon, Defensa 695, San Telmo
Tel: 4342 3700
Open: from 5pm. Closed Sundays.

This is the new version of Bar Seddon, where live bands play at weekends to a dedicated following of locals. It's about blues, jazz and the occasional rock act entertaining you while you sip your drink, but also about one of the iconic San Telmo bars that has made a miraculous recovery.

La Peña del Colorado, Güemes 3657, Palermo
Tel: 4822 1038 www.delcolorado.com.ar
Open: daily, noon (8pm Sun)–2am (5am Thurs–Sat)

La Peña del Colorado is a charming little place to drink *mate* (bitter green Argentine tea drunk through a straw, derived from the *mate* plant), listen to folklore, tango and jazz. Young, aspiring artists are regularly called up to strum, and there is a show of some sorts on every day from 10.30pm until midnight, by which time, it's hoped, you'll have moved on from the herbal tea.

Thelonious, Salguero 1884, Palermo

Tel: 4829 1562 www.thelonious.com.ar
Open: 9.30pm–4am Tues–Sat. Shows 10.30pm.

Palermo is apparently the jazz district of Buenos Aires. That is a bit of an exaggeration, but it was said with Thelonious, named after Thelonious Monk, in mind. Daily jazz sessions fill this bar with sax, drum and bass fans. Dinner at La Bourgogne's (see Eat) basement on a Friday night also feeds jazz cravings.

La Trastienda, Balcarce 460, San Telmo

Tel: 4342 7650 www.latrastienda.com.ar

With a 700 capacity, La Trastienda is big enough to create a head-banging atmosphere while small enough to keep it intimate. Many up-and-coming bands perform here, as well as established artists (there's a street market for both). Check the website for events at this San Telmo live lounge. Also see Notorious CD Bar, a record shop/cafe for more or look at website for details. (www.notorious.com.ar).

CASINOS

Casino Flotante de Buenos Aires, Dársena Sur, Elvira Rawson de Dellepiane, Puerto Madero

Tel: 4363 3100
Open: daily, 24 hours

The city and the government continue to fight over who should get the lion's share of the tax generated from the casino's current annual earnings of US$147 million. Open non-stop, there are 700 slot machines and 132 tables to lose your money at. Service is horribly slow at the tables, so do not expect Las Vegas-style treatment. For Texas Holdem' poker, head to the top floor of the boat.

Casino de Tigre, Peru 1385, Tigre
Tel: 4731 7000   www.trileniumcasino.com.ar
Open: 11am–4am Mon–Wed; 24 hours Thurs–Sun

A 40-minute drive from the centre of town, the Tigre Casino has 1,800 gaming machines and 74 tables (only one of which is poker). Cleaner and newer that the 'floating casino', Tigre opened in 2000; the floor is covered in blackjack and roulette tables and noisy slots. It claims to be South America's largest casino, and there is a hotel if things go well.

ADULT ENTERTAINMENT

FOR WOMEN:

Golden, Esmeralda 1040, Retiro
Tel: 4313 4323   www.golden.com.ar
Open: 11pm–5am. Closed Sundays.

Only for the eyes of the lady, Golden brings 500 square metres of strip club to Buenos Aires and plenty of naked, sculpted men, whose services are available at a price. Gigolos are a minority in Buenos Aires, as is whipped cream, which apparently Argentine girls love. Gentlemen, it's time to work on your six-packs.

FOR MEN:

Affaire, Affaire Pueyrredon 1114, Barrio Norte
www.affairebarrionorte.com
Open: daily, from 2pm

The girls will be kneeling on stools 'advertising' as you walk in to Affaire. Enough said. This is slightly better than Cocodrilo, although standards are not as at Madajos or Black; nevertheless, it is an entertaining place to have a drink, witness the Argentine addiction to brothels and to debate the insistence that it is okay to do it once in a while.

Black, corner of Ayacucho and Alvear, Recoleta
Tel: 4804 9652/9749
Open: from 11pm. Closed Sundays.

Opposite the Alvear Palace hotel and above Cartier, Black is the most exclusive of brothels in Buenos Aires. Inside it feels like a bar, or even a house party, in which there are around a hundred girls of different shapes and sizes, all of whom dress differently – some like saints and some like strippers – and all of whom are looking for the big-spending foreigner. If you are not here for the services and are religiously indifferent, the stripping nuns are highly entertaining.

Cocodrilo, Gallo 1311, Barrio Norte
Tel: 4963 7195
Open: daily, 10pm–7am

Diego Maradona's favourite, Cocodrilo is a household name in BA's brothel industry. Luckily you can go just for a drink and see what El Diego does in his spare time. Photos of him with his favourite girls are pinned up on the wall behind the bar, in front of which are a middle-of-the-range selection of strippers and professionals who pounce on foreigners.

Madajos, corner of Azcuenaga and Vincente Lopez, Recoleta
Tel: 4805 3208 /4807 1311

Less discreet than Black, but arguably better in terms of its personnel, Madajos is located beside the cemetery in Recoleta. You must buy the lady a drink – *una copa* – for around AR$30 if you want a serious conversation and around 20 times that if you want the conversation to go any further.

SHORT-STAY HOTELS (TELOS)

Argentines love their 'telos'. What is a 'telo'? A 'telo' is a slang word for hotel, the kind of hotel where you take a mistress, a lover, a girlfriend or boyfriend, or a professional lady of the night, just for a few hours.

General Paz Hotel, Av. General Paz 3921 y Monteagudo, Buenos Aires
Tel: 4752 0777 www.generalpazhotel.com
Price: AR$150–300

The General Paz Hotel is the most famous and exclusive of all the telos in Buenos Aires, and its rooms are more stylish than many of the rooms in the city's top, 'above board' hotels.

SWINGERS

Anchorena SW Club, Anchorena 1121 (corner of Paraguay), Barrio Norte
Tel: 15 6569 5215 www.anchorenasw.com
Open: from 11pm Fri–Sat
Price: Unaccompanied men AR$120; couples AR$50

Neon lights were invented for places like these. Swinging in Buenos Aires is more popular than you might think – most night-owls have been to a swingers' club at some time or another, and will admit it with a hint of gleeful shame. Anchorena is regarded to be the best of the bunch. Lord knows what the others must be like. This is a Roman-style orgy set out over three storeys. The first floor is home to the dance-floor, where Cumbia is pumped out, while a different sort of pumping occurs in the 'Couples Room' next door. Up one floor is the swimming-pool room with a bar, where couples go to negotiate the switch. Above this are two further salons where couples share the wipe-clean, white leather platforms and do their thing, while others sit around watching with a drink and ill-concealed arousal.

culture...

'*Buenos Aires siempre cambia*' – Buenos Aires is always changing. So the saying goes, and actually it's a pretty accurate description. Argentina has never really enjoyed a prolonged period of stability, and coupled with an enormously diverse mixture of immigrants, the country's culture continues to evolve.

Although Buenos Aires is packed with historical landmarks, you need to do more than a spot of sight-seeing to get a sense of the cultural heritage and life of the city: go for walks, and listen to and feel the bustling vibrancy the city emanates.

Buenos Aires was founded by gold prospectors in 1536, burned down by indigenous tribes in 1539 and rebuilt by Juan de Garay in 1580. During the 17th century, the indigenous population was 'controlled' and, despite attacks from the Dutch, French and Portuguese, the city remained under Spanish control until 25 May 1810, when the *porteños* forced the resignation of the Spanish viceroy and a provisional representative government was formed. Argentina's official independence on 9 July 1816 was finally declared following the revolts led by General Jose Francisco de San Martin, and the port of Buenos Aires became the country's capital.

In the late 19th century, foreign investors, among them the British, gradually came to Argentina, building railroads that reached out to the country's agricultural and cattle industries. Argentina began to enjoy a huge trade boom, sparking unprecedented levels of immigration from Europe.

With the indigenous peoples all but wiped out, thousands of Europeans poured off the boats, hoping to find the promised land. They were predominately Spaniards and Italians, but joining them were Croatian, British, French, German, Portuguese, Polish and Irish immigrants.

There are 48 *barrios* (neighbourhoods) in Buenos Aires, but you only need to experience a few to form a rounded picture of the city's culture.

Start with a trip to La Boca, where tango dancers, the old port and the Boca football stadium await you. El Caminito is where you need to begin your tour.

Next on the list is San Telmo, one of the oldest and best-preserved *barrios* in Buenos Aires, filled with colonial houses and cobblestone streets. Start with Plaza Dorrego in San Telmo and have a wander round.

Argentina's political hub is next. Plaza de Mayo, overlooked by the Casa Rosada, is the site of Argentina's finest and darkest hours, while the Palacio de Congreso is also a popular spot for the hundreds of protest marches – many funded by politicians – that take place.

In Retiro, take a look at the Torre de los Ingleses, which sits beside the Retiro railway station and in front of the Malvinas (Falklands) war memorial, behind Plaza San Martin. This will give you an idea of the extent of British influence in Buenos Aires.

We then move on to Recoleta, the richest area of the city, originally populated by those fleeing the 1871 yellow fever epidemic. This is where the city's most famous cemetery is to be found. Take a look at Evita's tomb before going on to the Museo de Bellas Artes.

Finally we move on to Palermo, a *barrio* divided into smaller areas. The best way to tackle Palermo is to walk up Avenida del Libertador and absorb the atmosphere of the museums and parks before arriving at Palermo Viejo, the old residential part of Palermo, where Buenos Aires' finest boutique shops are to be found.

When you've exhausted the sight-seeing, meet the Argentines to glean your best impression and understanding of this ever-changing society, whose culture is yet to be truly defined.

Avenida del Libertador

A walk up the Libertador from Recoleta is an experience you will not forget – you'll get to see enough sculptures and monuments for your entire trip. Start with Fernando Botero's Torso Masculino, a giant bronze sculpture with the largest buttocks in Buenos Aires (Plaza de Thays at Libertador and Schiaffino). Continue walking up the avenue before you hit Pueyrredon, where you must pop into the Museo de Bellas Artes. Next up is the

Facultad de Derecho (the law faculty), beside this sits Eduardo Catalano's Floralis Generica, a giant metallic flower that opens during the day and closes at night. Keep walking past the numerous statues and parks until you find the Museo de Arte Decorativo (see page 172), where you should stop for lunch at Croque Madame (see Snack). Cross back over to Figueroa Alcorta and you'll find the MALBA modern art gallery (see page 172). Keep on going up the avenue until you arrive at the Jardín Japonés (Japanese Gardens) (see page 167) and then finally reach Monumento a los Espanoles, where Avenida del Libertador hits Avenida Sarmiento.

La Boca

Some say the name 'La Boca' is derived from 'Boccadasse', an old sailor's neighbourhood of Genoa in Italy, from where many of the immigrants in the area came. Others say this working-class dockside area takes its name from its location at the mouth – la boca – of the river. It's a hard call. Either way, the area is famous for its multicoloured buildings – the inhabitants would scrounge paint from ships as they came into port – its passion for the tango, and its football. Having had lunch at El Obrero (see Snack), walk

down El Caminito, through the crowds of tango dancers and street salesman. Take a few pictures of the boats that float in the pungent water, sit down and watch the tango, and don't miss the Museo de Bellas Artes de la Boca Benito Quinquela Martin (see 172). There are cafés every-where, all similar in style and quality packed with tourists watching tango demonstrations. Go with the flow. Make sure you buy a Boca Juniors shirt and wear it to the game on the weekend. On your way back to your hotel, take a look at La Bombonera stadium and the Museo de la Pasion Boquense (Museum of Boca Passion – Brandsen 805; tel: 4362 1100, www.museoboquense.com; open: daily, 10am–7pm; closed on match days; guided tours hourly 11am to 5am), and remember: the policemen at the end of the tourist streets stop you passing into uncharted territory for a good reason.

La Casa Rosada and Plaza de Mayo, Congreso

Spanish for the 'Pink House', La Casa Rosada sits on the eastern side of the Plaza de Mayo. Completed in 1885, the palace is officially the seat of govern-ment, although the President lives in a more secure compound in the north-ern Olivos. Built on the foundations of a post office, a customs house and a fortress, La Casa Rosada overlooks the Plaza de Mayo, which is named after the month in 1810 when the First Council of Buenos Aires was sworn in (25 May). While the Cabildo is arguably the most important building in the square – this was the political nerve-centre from 1580 to 1821 – the Casa Rosada is the most famous. It has played host to the most joyful as well as the most distressing scenes in Argentina's history: from the crowds of ador-ing Eva Peron supporters, or Diego Maradona showing off the Jules Rimet

trophy after Argentina's 1986 World Cup victory, to President Fernando de La Rua's escape by helicopter from the palace's roof as the 2001/2 economic crash climaxed, provoking thousands of hungry Argentines to march onto the streets banging on saucepans, a scene which turned into a riot. A look at the Museo de la Casa Rosada (Hipolito Yrigoyen 21, tel: 4344 3802, www.museo.gov.ar) will fill you in.

Cementerio Recoleta

As ghost towns go, this is the world's number one. Presidents and a host of other important figures are buried here. Buried, however, is not the right word. This is a maze of private chapels in which the bodies are placed. Tourists now stroll up and down this luxurious cemetery, lined with marble mausoleums decorated with statues. Argentines love to be linear and the cemetery is laid out in grids, just like Buenos Aires. Eva Peron, former

presidents Carlos Pellegrini and Bartolomé Mitre, and Luis Firpo, a heavy-weight boxer known as 'the wild bull of the Pampas', are just some of the big names resting here.

Jardín Japonés, corner of Avenida Figueroa Alcorta and Avenida Casares, Palermo

Tel: 4804 4922/9141 www.jardinjapones.org.ar

Open: daily, 10am–6pm

The Japanese gardens have represented their community at the highest level in this Palermo neighbourhood. Designed by Yatuso Inomata in 1979 and donated to the Japanese community, the ornamental garden is best enjoyed

from the vantage of the red bridge that crosses the lake. Look out for the hungry carp who stick their heads out of the water, waiting to be fed.

Monumento a los Caidos Malvinas (Falklands Memorial), Retiro

The Falkands War was triggered by the Argentine invasion of South Georgia on 19 March 1982, presaging the imminent arrival of additional Argentine forces on the Falklands Islands. The justification for the invasion was that this was actually a reoccupation of Argentine land, given the proximity of the islands to Argentine shores – and the military government of the time, led by General Leopoldo Galtieri, saw this move as a way of boosting national pride amid a crippling economic crisis. The Argentine government did not believe the British would respond. Britain, however, led by Margaret

Thatcher, determined to defend British territory, and a naval task force was consequently assembled and sent to recapture the islands. Almost four months later, the war had claimed 907 lives, 258 of them British, and 649 of them Argentine. This memorial pays tribute to the hundreds of Argentine lives that were lost. Few Argentines bear a grudge against the English, although the English still complain about Diego Maradona's 'hand of God' goal in the 1986 World Cup quarter final in Mexico.

Plaza Dorrego, San Telmo

San Telmo is named after Pedro Gonzalez Telmo, a Roman Catholic priest from Astorga in Spain who converted locals to Christianity in the early 13th century. Although he was never canonized for his efforts, Pope Innocent IV beatified him eight years after his death, in 1254. San Telmo is one of the oldest parts of Buenos Aires, yet there are no specific monuments to visit. In terms of sightseeing, your best bet is to walk the crumbling streets and soak up the vibe. Plaza Dorrego is an ideal spot to sip on an afternoon shandy,

particularly on Sunday afternoon when the Feria de San Telmo attracts jewellery-makers and antique stalls surrounding the Plaza. The Plaza is over-looked by the blue-and-white-tiled Iglesia Nuestra Señora de Belén.

Plaza San Martin, Retiro

Plaza San Martin is named after General Jose Francisco de San Martin (1798–1850), who had a big hand in the independence of Argentina, Chile and Peru. Along with Simon Bolivar (1783–1830), San Martin is regarded to be one of the greatest liberators of South America, and as a result has been given the title of Padre de la Patria. Ironically, however, San Martin was exiled, and despite trying to return and fight for Argentina against Brazil, he died in France in 1850. The Plaza

San Martin is perhaps the most attractive of all the plazas in the city, and its bronze monument is one of the largest in the city.

Plazoleta Cortazar (Plaza Serrano), Palermo Viejo

Like San Telmo, Palermo Viejo is an old part of town, lacking any significant

sites, but it's best experienced on foot, especially if you love shopping! The one exception to this, however, is the Plazoleta Cortazar, better known as Plaza Serrano. The Plaza is a rounded market-place with swings in the middle, and an area for artists, jewellers and tradesmen to sell their goods. The weekends are packed with Argentines as well as tourists as there is so much going on in the area. El Ultimo Beso (Nicaragua 4880, tel: 4832 7711, www.elultimobeso.com.ar) is a couple of blocks away for afternoon tea.

Puerto Madero

The shallowness of the River Plate prevented large ships from docking at Buenos Aires' ports. In 1882 Julio Argentico Roca commissioned Eduardo Madero to construct a new port to solve the problem. The image of Buenos Aires was important to Roca's government, hence the insistence that the city had an accessible port. Construction began in 1887 and was completed in 1897. However, a decade later, the boats arriving at Buenos Aires became too large for the new Puerto Madero. The area fell into dereliction,  becoming one of the least savoury neighbourhoods, while a new port (Puerto Nuevo) was built and Puerto Madero was almost forgotten. Various regeneration strategies were planned over the years, but none was acted on until 1989, when an urbanization plan was set out for the area. Under Carlos Menem's government, Puerto Madero's facelift began. Billions of dollars have been and are still being spent on the docklands, and what was once a Mafia playground has become a contrived tourist hotspot. We don't really recommend you come to eat here at night (partying is fine though) – it's just too touristy – but a daytime walk around the docks and over the Puente de la Mujer, designed by Spanish architect Santiago Calatrava at a cost of six million dollars, is a relaxing, if not romantic experience.

Torre Monumental, Plaza Fuerza Aerea, Retiro
Tel: 4114 5791
Balcony open: noon–7pm Wed–Sat

Known as both the Torre Monumental and the Torre de los Ingleses, Buenos Aires' 'Big Ben' was donated by the city's British residents in 1910 to mark the 100-year anniversary of the May Revolutions. It is thought, however, that this gift was the British way of easing relations with the Argentines, who believed the British were exploiting them by exporting their beef and grain mountains (having built an advanced railway system from Retiro). The tower rises up in the middle of Plaza Fuerza Aerea ('Air Force Plaza') opposite the Retiro railway station. The clock at the top of the tower is made in the form of an Elizabethan frigate and visitors can take a lift to the top of the tower to look over Plaza San Martin and the Monumento

a Los Caidos Malvinas, which was purposely built – in an act of defiance from the Argentines – in front of the tower following the 1982 Falklands War. The tower was renamed the Torre Monumental by the Argentines (all British monuments were renamed after the war), although it is still called la Torre de los Ingleses by *porteños*.

THEATRES

Teatro Colón, Cerrito, between Tucuman and Viamonte
Tel: 4378 7344   www.teatrocolon.org.ar
Open: 9am–5pm Mon–Fri

The Colón's construction began in 1889 under the supervision of architect Francesco Tamburini and his pupil Angelo Ferrari. However, it took a further 20 years for the theatre to be completed after planning issues marred the project. Julio Dormal finished the job and the theatre opened on 25 May

1908 with a performance of Verdi's *Aida*. Since then the Colón has attracted most of the world's leading talents, including Luciano Pavarotti. The frescos on the cupola, painted by Raul Soldi, and the scarlet and gold décor, ensure that the Colón is as beautiful as it sounds: the acoustics are thought to be the third best in the world, after the opera houses in Paris and Vienna, and, interestingly, the stage flips around right under the Avenida 9 de Julio. In addition to opera, ballet legends such as Alicia Alonso, Margot Fonteyn, Paloma Herrera and Julio Bocca have danced here.

ART GALLERIES

MALBA – (Museo de Arte Latinoamericano de Buenos Aires), Avenida Figueroa Alcorta 3415, Palermo
Tel: 4808 6500   www.malba.org.ar
Open: noon–8pm (9pm Weds). Closed Tuesdays.

MAMBA (Museo de Arte Moderno de Buenos Aires), San Juan 350, San Telmo
Tel: 4361 1121   www.aamamba.org.ar
Open: 10am (11am Sat–Sun)–8pm. Closed Mondays.

Museo de Arte Decorativo, Av. del Libertador 1902, Palermo
Tel: 4802 6606 / 4801 8248 / 4806 8306   www.mnad.org
Open: 2pm–7pm. Closed Mondays (and Sundays in Jan/Feb).

Museo de Bellas Artes de la Boca Benito Quinquela Martin, Avenida Pedro de Mendoza 1835, La Boca
Tel: 4301 1080
Open: 11am–5pm Tues–Fri; 11am–5.30pm Sat–Sun. Closed January.

Museo Fernandez Blanco, Suipacha 1422, Recoleta
Tel: 4327 0272 / 0228
Open: 2–7pm. Closed Mondays. Holidays open 3–7pm.

Museo Nacional de Bellas Artes, Avenida del Libertador 1473, Recoleta
Tel: 4803 0802 / 4691 www.mnba.org.ar
Open: 12.30–7pm Tues–Fri; 9.30am–7.30pm Sat–Sun

PRIVATE GALLERIES

Jorge Mara, La Ruche, Arenales 1321, Recoleta
Tel: 4813 0552 www.laruche.com.ar

Focusing on young, genuinely talented artists, Jorge Mara has found a niche in the Argentine market.

Marcos Bledel, Cerrito 1332, Recoleta
Tel: 4815 0274 / 4813 6158 www.marcosbledel.com

Argentina's leading expert in *gaucho* art, Marcos Bledel is the main distributor of Molino Campos paintings, as well as 19th-century European paintings.

Niko Gulland, Bulnes 2241, Palermo
Tel: 4822 2064 / 4802 2479 / 15 4446 2479 www.nikogulland.com

Niko Gulland sells contemporary Argentine art from a small Palermo office.

Renoir Galeria de Arte, Arroyo 840, Retiro
Tel: 4327 0678 / 15 5610 9191 (cell) www.galeriarenoir.com.ar

Despite the name, the Renior gallery focuses on 'River Plate' art, selling both Argentine and Uruguayan artists.

shop...

'Lo bueno del hacer shopping en Buenos Aires es que para todo el mundo es regalado!' This essentially means – given the weakness of the devalued Argentine peso – shopping is dirt cheap for foreigners.

Because of the bargain free-for-all, you'll spend as much as you would in any other city, but your suitcases will be weighed down with cutting-edge fashion. And with many shops offering tax-free incentives, you might be able to afford more than a cup of coffee in the departure lounge after 21% of your fashion spend has been refunded at the airport's Puesto de Pago booth.

So what is on offer and where do you find it?

Given that image, looks and attitude are paramount in BA, you can take it as read that fashion is of unparalleled importance – indeed, the city has a wide selection of boutiques catering to everyone's whims, although it takes some time to master the unique *porteño* attitude. Bear in mind that Argentines are renowned for their rake-thin figures, so if you do eat three meals a day, perhaps you ought to rethink before you arrive in Buenos Aires if you want to squeeze into the jeans: for girls, Rapsodia and Jazmin Chebar are extremely hip at the moment.

Where should you go? Argentina's up-and-coming – for a reason – independent designers generally open up shop in the cobbled street catwalk of the regenerated Palermo Viejo. Cafés and chic restaurant/bars line the streets, giving shoppers cause for a break for lunch. From chic and retro to urban and classic, every style is available for the constantly fickle fashion-conscious. Our list represents the latest in Argentine design, but check our website for updates. Palermo Viejo is the fashionable *porteña's* first port of call for shopping in BA, so ignore any advice pointing you in the direction of Florida Street or the Micro Centro.

If you're not into browsing, exploring and window shopping, then the shopping centres, in particular Paseo Alcorta and Alto Palermo, will be of help. They include the most successful Argentine brands, as well as some international names. 'Shoppings' are a gathering point for *porteñas*, who adore flicking through the racks and cooling down in the air-conditioned balconies of the malls, which also include fast-food restaurants and sometimes cinemas.

Back down in Recoleta, the elegant Avenida Alvear is home to international designers such as Luis Vuitton, Armani, Ferragamo, Hermès and Ralph Lauren. Most of these aren't listed in the following pages, since we've decided they can play second fiddle to the home-grown talent. So have a wander up the Avenida Alvear, which takes five minutes, to peruse the international boutiques and global fashionistas.

Moving away from fashion, for art you need to head to Arroyo Street, although Cerrito Street's Marcos Bledel is the world's top gallery for *gaucho* art, with the largest collection of Molino Campos paintings. Although San Telmo is renowned for its antiques shops — and it is worth a stroll — the selection of stores in the Recoleta area is generally of higher quality. Finally, leather. We have listed a couple of stores to accommodate your particular fetish; as a rule of thumb the outlets in shopping malls are more expensive and of a lower standard than the boutique leather stores around town.

ARMENIA

Anahi M (1490) – bags and pocket books for busy city girls (www.anahi-m.com.ar)

Charlotte Solnicki (1577) – chic and glam womenswear ideal for the Buenos Aires party scene, now sold in London, New York and Los Angeles (www.charlottesolnicki.com)

Mariana Toledo (1564) – ultra-boutique women's dresses, wedding gowns included (www.marianotoledo.com.ar)

La Merceria (1609) – fashionable lifestyle accessories to wear and for the home

Sibyl Vane (1670) – shoes and avant-garde accessories (www.sibylvane.com)

EL SALVADOR

Amor Latino (4813) – sensual lingerie for the girl around town

Chibel (4611) – colourful, well-designed and well-cut children's clothing (www.chibel.com)

Cora Groppo (4696) – cute dresses, skirts and blouses with an urban touch

Divia (6033) – sophisticated exotic and delicate shoes, *hechos a medida*

Eufemia (4601) – independent, rebellious and sexy range of urban womenswear

Hermanos Estebecorena (5960) – men's clothes with a hip industrial edge (www.hermanosestebecorena.com)

Humawaca (4692) – 100% Argentine leather (www.humawaca.com)

Jazmin Chebar (4702) – relaxed and formal clothes in a French-style boutique from one of Argentina's top designers (www.jazminchebar.com.ar)

Juana de Arco (4762) – playful lingerie, and colourful and fun summer clothing (www.juanadearco.net)

Maria Cher (4724) – for feminine, independent and free-spirited young women

Mishka (4673) – shoes for princesses

Varanasi (4761) – prêt-à-porter fashion with a touch of Indian spice

GORRITI

Balthazar (5131) – cutting-edge men's clothes for every occasion
Deberser (5876) – men's clothing with an edgy, underground design
(www.deberser.com)
Milagros (5417) – romantic furniture for the newly wed
Santorini (4849) – modern furniture for the ultimate playboy pad
(www.santorini.com.ar)

GURRUCHAGA

Bolivia (1581) – wacky, colourful shirts, stripy trousers and jackets for
men (www.boliviaonline.com.ar)
El Cid (1732) – men's clothes range, from velvet trousers to preppy, long-
sleeved T-shirts (www.el-cid.com.ar)
Felix (1670) – relaxed and casual men's clothing range
Marcelo Senra (1519) – range from a designer who considers the architecture of women's bodies when creating a garment
(www.marcelosenra.com)
Qara (1548) – expensive handbags, purses and luggage for both men and
women
Santillan (1638) – boutique selling handmade swimsuits and casual wear
alongside beautiful handmade accessories (www.santillanbsas.com)
Satori (1538) – everyday shoes for men and women
(www.satorishoes.com.ar)
Simple (2181) – high-quality designer furniture and harmoniously contemporary objects (www.simpledecoonline.com.ar)
Sylo (1624) – jackets, trousers, shirts and belts for the less-conservative
conservative (www.sylobsas.com)

HONDURAS

Desiderata (4733) – hip and urban dresses, shorts and jackets for the
Punta crowd (www.desiderata.com.ar)

Mancini (5140) – clothes and luggage for both men and women

Mariana Dappiano (4932) – an eclectic collection of 'smart sports' clothing

Salsipuedes (4814) – fun but cheap accessories, including fishing-line necklaces and plastic bangles from the 1960s

Uma (5225) – jeans and accessories for women (www.umacuero.com)

Urano (4702) – Argentine design for an ever-changing, modern world (www.uranodesing.com)

Vevu (4829) – divas and their daughters unite in this Palermo Viejo boutique

SOLER

A.Y. Not Dead (4193) – men's and woman's funk named after Mafia boss Alfredo Yabran (www.aynotdead.com.ar)

Denim Center (4202) – national and international range of jeans, accessories, sunglasses and cowboy boots (www.denim-center.com)

Velas de la Ballena (4802) – the best candles and handcrafted soaps in the city

THAMES

Bendita Tu Eres (1555) – underwear for sassy Argentine girls

Fight For Your Right (1425) – an alternative take on men's urbanwear: caps, hoodies, T-shirts and sunglasses (www.fightnet.com.ar)

Infinit (1602) – contemporary and stylish range of sunglasses for men and women (www.infinitnet.com)

Wool (1891) – rugs and contemporary home products (www.alfombras-wool.com)

ELSEWHERE

Babel (Serrano 1542) – home decoration, funky lampshades, fabric, rugs and furniture (www.babelartesyoficios.com)

Cuartaflor (Uriarte 1456) – up-and-coming chic design for most women

Freak (Niceto Vega 5254) – chic bags and purses nestled away in Palermo Hollywood

Grisino (Malabia 1784) – playful designer wear for women out to break the mould (www.grisino.com.ar)

Los Vados del Isen (Aráoz 2918, Palermo) – great accessories with original designs

STORES

La Corte Vintage (Nicaragua 5999) – vintage-cut suits in an English style for men

Manifesto (Humboldt 2160) – modern furniture with a classic design (www.clasicosmodernos.com)

Pasion Argentina (Ravignani 1780) – deco leather, clothes and art

Rapsodia (Arguibel 2899, Las Cañitas) – jeans designed to enhance your figure to its maximum (www.rapsodia.com.ar)

AVENIDA ALVEAR

La Dolfina (1315) – Adolfo Cambiasso's clothing line for polo players and groupies (www.ladolfina.com)

Dot Store (1516) – high-fashion, boutique women's line from a burgeoning Argentine designer

Hieber (1640) – luxury handbags and accessories. You need to press the bell to enter (www.hieber.com.ar).

Lonté (1814) – high-quality handmade shoes from two Italian brothers

Perugia Bottier (1862) – chic shoes in an elegant neighbourhood

AVENIDA SANTA FE

Claude Benard (1583) – chic shoes for stylish girls
Paula Cahen Danvers (1619) – fabulous women's clothes, a favourite
with the society girls

LIBERTAD

De Maria (1661) – designer shoes with understated elegance
L'Ecat (1360) – amazing selection of antiques
Luna Garzón (1185) – classically designed jewellery and accessories
María Vázquez (1632) – One of Argentina's most famous models brings
you her designs. Her dresses are fabulous.
Vetmas (1276) – one of Recoleta's finest antique stores, well worth a visit

QUINTANA

Ben Simon (492) – preppy men's clothes with attitude
Sathya (53) – evening wear and dancing clothes

ELSEWHERE

30 Yardas (French 2426) – Eduardo Heguy uses 30 yards sticks. This is a
growing saddlery and is the best for polo equipment in the city
(www.30yardas.com).
Aracano (Luis Agote 2388) – Collection of silver objects inspired from
Native Argentine designs. Bold, elegant and unique pieces are created from
sterling silver combined with horn and leather. Special gold pieces are made
on commission. The Aracano studio can be visited by appointment only (tel:
4803 0304).
Benito Fernandez (Arroyo 894) – snappy yet elegant dresses and wedding gowns (www.benitofernandez.com.ar)
Breeder's (Posadas 1269) – skins, rugs, shawls and accessories for
sophisticated ladies
Chucker (Galileo 2430) – polo gear for real polo players
(www.chucker.com.ar)

Della Signoria (Arroyo 971) – one of BA's top antique shops
Etiqueta Negra (Unicenter, Paseo Alcorta) – formal, stylish and preppy clothing using dark colours
Prüne (Florida 963, Centre) – beautiful handbags, shoes, leather goods and other accessories
Rambo (Ayacucho 1974) – fine selection of antiques (www.ramboantiques.com)
Tramando (Rodríguez Peña 1973) – Martín Churba creates objects, intertwining and weaving recycled remnants of the textile industry
Trosman (Avenida del Libertador 750) – edgy, avant-garde, chic design for women in a range of unusual and inventive materials (www.trosman.com)

REST OF BUENOS AIRES

STORES

Almacen Cabrini (Cabrera 3955) – Deco design for your home. Good for gifts and one-off items.
Antilope (Hipolito Yrigoyen 847, Aveilaneda) – BA's best underground leather and fur factory outlet, high quality individual pieces are made to order (www.cuerosframar.com.ar)
Pablo Ramirez (Peru 587, San Telmo) – passionate about retro and black fabric, Pablo brings high style to San Telmo

PERSONAL SHOPPERS

Planners & Co
Tel: 4816 6529   www.plannersandco.com

While Leila and Victoria pull off that Buenos Aires fashion-clad, society-girl image, they have much more of an adventurous edge to them than most personal shoppers, which is why their services are in high demand. Born and raised in Buenos Aires' shopping malls, they now dedicate their time to professional credit-card bashing. They will take you off the beaten shopping routes, into the factories, join you in the fitting rooms and will work to your budget. You are in good hands. From US$30 an hour.

Estefania Allende
tefina@hotmail.com

Estefania, or Tefi as she likes to be called, is one of Buenos Aires' top stylists and picks most of the outfits you see paraded on Buenos Aires' billboards. She thrives on meeting foreigners looking to fit into the Buenos Aires fashion scene, so take her advice. You can email her for an appointment, and don't be put off by her hotmail address – she refuses to get a more serious email.

SHOPPING CENTRES

Alto Palermo, Santa Fe 3253, Palermo
Tel: 5777 8000 www.altopalermo.com.ar
Open: daily, 10am–10pm

Also accessed on Coronel Diaz and Arrenales, Alto Palermo is the most fashionable of Buenos Aires' shopping malls. Located in the centre of Palermo, the mall is frequented by a hip *porteño* crowd, who pop in on their way back from work in the evening, while trendy youths with time on their hands stroll up and down looking for new outfits for Buenos Aires' electric nightlife.

Paseo Al Corta, Salguero 3172, Palermo
Tel: 5777 6500
Open: daily, 10am–10pm

Paseo Al Corta has slightly better shops than Alto Palermo, but is not as centrally located. Nevertheless, it's worth making the trip up here. This is the most serious shopping centre for clothes in the city, and it's regarded as the most complete by Buenos Aires' demanding shopaholics.

Patio Bullrich, Posadas 1245, Recoleta
Tel: 4814 7400 www.shoppingbullrich.com.ar
Open: daily, 10am–9pm

The choice of the elegant Recoleta ladies, located in front of the Caesar Park Hotel, and for a reason: the shops are perhaps the most sophisticated in BA. Wealthy locals like to congregate for a cup of coffee in the early evenings after a spot of window-shopping. The centre also contains a cinema.

play...

It has been said Buenos Aires offers limitless possibilites for nocturnal indulgence, but little in terms of daytime activities once you've soaked up the culture and bought yourself a new wardrobe. There is an element of truth in this, but only if you compare what's on offer in this bustling metropolis to Argentina's vast land mass which, at 2.7 million square kilometres, is the second largest in South America after Brazil, making this the eighth biggest playground in the world.

Argentina is a plain, sandwiched between the Atlantic Ocean to the east, and the Andes to the west. To the north, swamps, deserts, lush valleys and jungles make up the terrain, while to the south is Patagonia, a region of cool, arid steppes, deserts and forests at the foot of the Andes. Buenos Aires province is the most hospitable of all the terrains, and it's hard to imagine the contrasting landscapes that make up this country while you're here.

Whether it's *gauchos* roaming the pampas, the highest mountain outside Asia, volcanoes, the continent's only advancing glaciers, waterfalls bigger than Niagara, crystal-clear lakes, Argentina's wildlife, or rivers swarming with trout

that intrigue you, Buenos Aires happens to be perfectly placed for you to access all of this.

With regular internal flights around the country, you are only three and a half hours – the time it takes for dinner, a couple of drinks and a dance – from the southernmost city in the world (Ushuaia, in Tierra del Fuego), two and a half hours from the Iguazu Falls in Misiones, and an hour and a half – a stroll around Palermo Viejo's shops – from the ski slopes in the Neuquen and Mendosa provinces.

Could it get much better? you may ask yourself. With two of the planet's most pulsating soccer stadiums, the most important polo ground in the world, and a 100,000-seat racecourse within the city, the answer is yes. If you're a sportsman, start stretching immediately, and if you're an armchair specialist then order your match programme.

Now consider that Buenos Aires' climate means that wetsuits are not necessary when wakeboarding on the Tigre delta, and that it seldom rains enough to stop you playing on the dozens of golf courses and polo grounds on the periphery of the city. The wind does occasionally get up, however, filling the sails of the yachts on the River Plate.

Estancia San Pedro, Cañuelas, Ruta 3, Km 50
Tel: 15 4162 7795

There are over 1,000 head of cattle for you to corral at Estancia San Pedro. A visit here will provide as penetrating an insight into the life of a South American cowboy, the *gaucho*, as you will find. While modern times have seen the *gaucho* culture diluted, these cattle herders are as close to the real thing as you will get. After herding in the cattle (and seeing an Argentine milk farm in action), the *paesanos* will teach you how to cook an authentic Argentine barbecue. Ask for Nicolas Fiorito when organizing the day. Nicolas also arranges polo at the neighbouring farm La Totona Polo Club (La Totona Polo Club, Cañuelas, Provincia de Buenos Aires, Ruta 3 Km 50, tel: 15 6162 7795, www.totona.com.ar).

CLIMBING

Las Taguas, Carlos Pellegrini 1135
Tel: 5032 0042   www.lastaguas.com

Aconcagua – At 6,959 metres, the Andes' Aconcagua is the highest peak in the world outside Asia. In 2000 Italians Bruno Bronod, Fabio Meralsi and Jean Pellissier, all in their late 20s and 30s, broke the record for the fastest ascent from the Plaza de Mulas base camp (at 4,300 metres) to the summit with a time of 3 hours 40 minutes. The group acclimatized for 10 days at Plaza de Mulas before racing up to the top. They spent just 5 minutes at the summit before descending in 72 minutes. The previous record, set in 1992 by French mountaineers, was achieved in 4 hours 36 minutes. We don't expect you to beat the Italians, although we wouldn't mind if you did. Contact Las Taguas tourism before leaving for Argentina to select the best guides for your needs.

Lanin Volcano – Ten thousand years have passed since the last eruption of the Lanin Volcano, close to San Martin de Los Andes in Patagonia, so it's more likely you'll be injured by falling boulders than molten lava if you stray onto the glacier. Your guide will take you up to the 3,776-metre summit over two days, and you'll spend a breathtaking night in one of the mountainside shelters. The views of the lakes around San Martin de Los Andes and the neighbouring volcanoes are incredible, and the deep blue colour of the lakes becomes richer the higher you climb. With the right guide, you can attempt the Lanin in one day. The official record stands at around 5 hours 30 minutes. Our record is 6 hours 35 minutes. Had we had more Gatorade, this time could have been improved.

COCKTAIL-SHAKING

Tato
Tel: 15 6761 2908 (cell) renato_tato@yahoo.com

Tato is widely considered to be Buenos Aires' finest barman. Having worked in New York and in Europe, this tattooed and devilishly sexy man has gained international recognition, and as a result was given the call by Terry Walshe at Club 647, the most exclusive members club in Buenos Aires. He loves to shake, slice and proclaim 'grosso', which in this context means 'fantastic'. He has built a new bar at his house and will instruct you in the ways of a cocktail master. The price of the class (US$75–200) depends on what liquor is used and how much he likes you.

COOKERY

Rodrigo Toso, Caesar Park Hotel, Recoleta
Tel: 4819 1182   chef.cpba@caesar.com.ar
US$70–100

Rodrigo Toso, chef at the Agraz (see Eat), offers cooking classes at his Caesar Park Hotel base. As well as offering private tutorials, he will teach groups of up to 40 how to flash their pans. Rodrigo is widely regarded as one of the finest chefs in the city, and this Recoleta kitchen is easy to get to. For an extravagant day's cooking on the Tigre delta, it doesn't get much better – or pricier – than this. Allow yourself to be picked up in a car, and driven to the docks where your group will board a 1945 wooden motor yacht formerly owned by five-times Formula One champion Juan Manuel Fangio. You will then be taken to an island on the Tigre delta where you will learn how to cook Argentine beef the Argentine way, and chef up more compli-cated, gourmet dishes. It is also possible to be taken by helicopter – just ask Rodrigo to set it up. A group of 20 will cost US$3,500–5,500, depending on transport, smaller groups are negotiable.

CRICKET

Although this is an Argentine town, the English will be English and continue to churn out the crustless cucumber sandwiches. The ex-pat contingent is still strong in Buenos Aires, and the cricketing community, although suffering from transport restrictions when trying to get hold of the necessary kit, still has four teams in the 'First Division'. The main two clubs are the Belgrano Athletic Club and the Hurlingham Club, although Lomas is on the up. Call them up to watch a game or challenge one of their XIs to a limited over game. The pitches are dry with plenty of foot holes, ripe for a spinner. The Argentine Cricket Association's website is www.cricketargentina.com (tel: 4816 3569).

Belgrano Athletic Club, Virrey del Pino 3456, Belgrano
Tel: 4552 2259/2094 www.belgrano-athletic.com.ar

Founded in 1896, the Belgrano Athletic Club is the only cricket club in the centre of Buenos Aires. Although it is surrounded by apartment buildings, the clubhouse itself could not be any more English. Like the Hurlingham Club, it is always open to touring sides, and the tea ladies are perhaps even more efficient than back in Blighty. Given that this is a rugby pitch in the winter, the outfield can be a little bumpy.

Hurlingham Cricket Club, Avenida Julio A. Roca 1411, Hurlingham
Tel: 4662 5510 www.hurlinghamclub.org.ar

Founded in 1888, by whom else but the English, the Hurlingham Club is per-haps the most elite club in Argentina – and they are proud of it. Old Etonian Clem H. Gibson is the club's most famous medium-paced swing and seam bowler, who graced the field in the 1920s and '30s. Hurlingham's pool of players is desperate to play touring sides.

DJ CLASSES

Sonica, Avenida Elcano 3835/37, Buenos Aires
Tel: 4551 7924 www.escuelasonica.com.ar

Buenos Aires loves its electronic beats. DJ-ing, Advanced DJ-ing, DJ-ing on a computer and advice on how to MC a killer show of your own is all on offer here. Your first class will start with a beat session. Given that DJs are somewhat nocturnal, at Sonica the lesson times are flexible. Courses can be anything up to three months long, depending on how keen you are.

FISHING

Arroyo Verde Lodge, Bariloche, Rio Negro Province

This luxurious lodge is nestled in the Traful Valley overlooking Lake Traful, the source of the river that runs beautifully through it, and holds all different kinds of 'salmonids': rainbow, brown and brook trout and the occasional land-locked salmon.

Bella Vista Lodge, Santa Cruz Province

This *estancia* is situated on the Rio Gallegos, where sea-run and dry-fly brown trout fishing can be enjoyed. It owns nearly 50km of double bank private access fishing, which is limited to a maximum of eight rods per week.

Kau Tapen Lodge, Tierra del Fuego

Kau Tapen is generally considered to be one of the finest fly-fishing lodges in the world. Excellent food and attentive service complement a top-class sea-trout fishing experience on the Rio Grande in remote and idyllic surroundings.

Lago Villarino Lodge, San Martin de los Andes, Neuquen Province

This lodge is located slap bang in the middle of Nahuel Huapi National Park,

50km from San Martin de Los Andes. The brown trout are large to say the least, and are more attracted to a sinking fly than the floating mosca.

Pira Lodge, Corrientes Province

The world's first deluxe lodge to fish the freshwater dorado. Corrientes is in the middle of the Iberá marshland; covering an area of 3,200,000 acres, the marsh is one of the largest and most diverse wetlands in the world.

Tipiliuke Lodge, Junin de los Andes, Neuquen Province

Everything is arranged for fly fisherman to have an unforgettable trout fishing trip – it includes specialized guides, vehicles, outdoor lunches, and trips to nearby rivers and lakes. Fishing programmes focus on the lodge's private stretch of the famous Chimehuin River.

The people to contact to organize fishing trips are Argentina Outfitters (tel: 5032 0042 www.argentinaoutfitters.com) trips are run by Hale Snyder (hale@argentinaoutfitters.com).

FOOTBALL

Football is the favourite, the second favourite and the third favourite sport in Argentina. Football is passion. Take the time to see at least one game during your trip. The season is split into two: the 'apertura' (opening), which begins in August and climaxes in December, and the 'clausura' (closing), which runs from February to July, while the Copa Libertadores runs through the winter months until July, depending on the season and how many games are postponed due to crowd violence. GoFootball (see below) will take you to the games in safety – believe us when we say that Argentine stadiums are dangerous and intimidating places. Alternatively, use Ticketek (tel: 5237 7200, www.ticketek.com.ar) to book your own tickets. Never go to a ground and buy a seat in the 'popular' stands, unless you want to the game to be your last. The 'platea' seats are the ones for the peaceful fan.

GoFootball
Tel: 4816 2618 or 15 4405 9526 www.gofootball.com.ar

This is the safe way to go to a game. GoFootball will pick you up from your hotel in an air-conditioned van with other tourists, take you through the crowds, and then babysit you before, during and after the game. We like this company because they offer a wider range of games, not just the usual Boca or River games. Whether it's a River Plate, Boca Juniors, Racing, Independiente, San Lorenzo or Velez game, you will be looked after. If they are all booked up, then contact Las Taguas (tel: 5032 0042, www.lastaguas.com), who will find you tickets and a personal guide.

Boca Juniors, Estadio Alberto J Armando (La Bombonera), Brandsen 805, La Boca

Tel: 4309 4700 www.bocajuniors.com.ar

'*La Bombonera no tiembla… late*' ('The sweet shop does not shake, rather it beats like a heart'). If this stadium doesn't get your blood boiling, then nothing will. Boca Juniors are the people's team in Argentina and their stadium, La Bombonera ('The Sweet Shop'), is unquestionably the loudest and most passionate sporting arena in Argentina. The name of Diego Maradona – who still attends games regularly and sits in a box with yellow seats above the halfway line – is still chanted before most games by the Xeneize (Boca fans). 'They can gas and hit us, but we will always be by your side,' is one line of one of their songs, which never cease throughout the game. '*El que no salta es un Ingles*' ('Whoever doesn't jump up and down is an Englishman') is another one to listen out for if your cover is not to be blown. Boca have won more international titles than any other team, including Real Madrid and AC Milan, winning five Copa Libertadores and three World Club Crowns. Carlos Bianchi is Boca's most successful coach, with seven Argentine league titles and eight international titles.

River Plate, Avenida Figueroa Alcorta 7597, Núñez

Tel: 4789 1200 www.cariverplate.com.ar

Having allegedly lost a game to Boca Juniors to decide which team would stay in the area of La Boca, River Plate moved upmarket towards Palermo, and finally to Núñez. 'River' now play at the Estadio Monumental, where Argentina won the 1978 World Cup. Because of the athletics track, the seats are a little too far away from the pitch, but when filled with 60,000 fans, the atmosphere is electric, especially at a '*superclasico*' encounter against rivals Boca Juniors. River have won 32 national league titles and have claimed the title three years in a row, a feat that Boca Juniors – to the delight of River fans – have never achieved. River supporters are nicknamed the '*gallinas*' (chickens), while the team are known as the '*millonarios*' (millionaires) because this is a posh neighbourhood. Club legends include Enzo Francescoli (El Principe), Ariel Ortega (El Burrito), Javier Saviola (El Conejito) and Marcelo Salas (El Matador). Other interesting topics: turncoat Gabriel Batistuta (Batigol) played for both Boca and River; plus, Diego Maradona almost played for River Plate before he moved to Boca Juniors from the Argentina Juniors – not that Boca fans like to admit it.

GLACIERS

Las Taguas, Carlos Pellegrini 1135, Buenos Aires
Tel: 5032 0042 www.lastaguas.com

After you've seen the Iguazu Falls, you'll think Argentina is just showing off with its glaciers. The jewel in the crown is the Perito Moreno Glaciar. Measuring 250 square km, and 30km long, it is one of 48 glaciers fed by the Southern Patagonian Ice Field but only one of three Patagonian glaciers that aren't retreating. Impressive chunks of ice crash down into the water from a height of 60 metres, below which are a further 170 metres of ice. The glacier advances (and retreats) at a rate of 2 metres a day. Visitors can walk on the ice further up the glacier, and there are boat trips around other glaciers in the area. Stay at the new Esplendor Hotel when in El Calafate (see Sleep), or at Los Notros (www.losnotros.com), which is the only hotel within the national park.

GOLF

Buenos Aires Golf Course, Mayorlirsuta 3777, Bella Vista
Tel: 4468 1696/1693 www.bagolf.com.ar

Just half an hour away from Recoleta, this big dog in Buenos Aires' golf scene was designed by the Houston-based firm of Robert von Hagge, with Kelly Blake Moran as the chief architect. The club's reputation was boosted by hosting the 2000 EMC World Cup, when Tiger Woods and David Duval took the spoils for the USA. This course is very American, but provides an undeniably challenging round of golf.

Jockey Club, Avenida Marquez 1700, San Isidro
Tel: 4743 1001/1678 www.jockeyclub.com.ar

The 1962 and 1970 World Cup competitions were hosted here. Originally a flat, marshy area, Allister Mackenzie – who designed the Augusta National, Royal Melbourne and Crystal Downs – created this course despite a lack of ground-moving equipment. There are two courses, the 'Cancha Colorada' at 6,060 metres, and the 'Azul' at 5,695 metres, both par 72, and both inaugurated in 1928. Mounds, bunkers and contouring were built so that every hole has a slight trick.

Olivos, Ruta Panamericana Ramal Pilar, KM 32, Ramal Pilar
Tel: 4463 1076/0035 www.olivosgolf.cc

Founded in 1926, apparently Olivos Golf Club's course is better than the Jockey Club's. It has 27 holes (originally 36), and was designed by the Englishmen who built Argentina's railroads; it is well bunkered, incorporating plenty of water traps and a lot of rough, as well as mature trees that line the fairways. Keep your eye on the ball and pray you hit it straight.

La Orquídea, Ruta 6, Camino Capilla del Señor, Cardales
Tel: 02322 493537/493674 www.laorquidea.com.ar
Open: Mon, Thur, Fri, Sat and Sun. Tuesday and Wednesday are group days.

Opened in 1991, La Orquídea is one of the new clubs to have built a reputation fast. A Federico Bauer and Federico Maurer creation, there are three courses here: the Red, the White and the Blue. The youngest of our selection, La Orquídea is a modern course; we'll leave it up to you to decide whether you like it.

Driving Range, Avenida Rafael Obligado, Costanera Norte
Tel: 4801 9245/4305
Bucket of 60 balls: $5

Fly Ranch, Public Aerodrome Gomez, Route 2, KM 65
Tel: 15 5249 9282 www.flyranch.com.ar

The good news is that if you do have to crash-land from a height of 700 metres, all the terrain here is as flat as a pancake, so you only have to worry about squashing cows and *gauchos*. Fly Ranch works as a hang-gliding school, offering classes for beginners and DragonFly and trike aerotowing for the more experienced. No need to book a car from your hotel – they will organize everything.

Patagonia Chopper Flight Tours
Tel: 4795 6410 or 15 5662 0283 www.patagoniachopper.com.ar

This is the only company in Buenos Aires offering helicopter tours in and around the city, as well as point-to-point travel in a range of private helicopters and private jets. The aerial tours are surprisingly cheap (starting from US$111), while a trip over the Tigre delta costs from US$85. Why not take a trip to the Delta and have lunch at Lima Limo (see Snack).

They always seem to be racing in Buenos Aires. The Palermo track sits in front of the polo ground and the 100,000-seat stadium is visible as you drive into town from Figueroa Alcorta. Saturdays, Sundays and Mondays are race days in Palermo, while Wednesdays, Saturdays and Sundays are race days at San Isidro. San Isidro hosts the Carlos Pellegrini in December, a meeting definitely not to be missed.

Hipódromo Argentino de Palermo, Avenida del Libertador 4101, Palermo
Tel: 4778 2800 www.palermo.com.ar

Hipódromo de San Isidro, Avenida Marquez 504, San Isidro

Tel: 4743 4019/4011 www.hipodromosanisidro.com.ar

HORSE-RIDING IN THE PATAGONIAN ANDES

Argentina Outfitters

Tel: +5411 5032 0042 www.argentinaoutfitters.com

Patrick Steverlylynck, whose family owns one of the only private estates in the national park, will take you on an eight-day trip on horseback through the foothills of the Andes. You will start at Lago Hermoso – a private 14,000-acre ranch – and continue into the mountains, cross river fords and traverse remote trails. The views are spectacular. Evenings are spent beside lakes and rivers by the fire. Inflatable mattresses are not provided.

HUNTING

DOVE-SHOOTING

Las Colas Lodge, Gualeguay, Entre Ríos Province

Contact: Rob McAndrew – rmcandrew@argentinaoutfitters.com

Full-day dove-shoots with early-morning departures and same-day return to the city. This ranch is located in Entre Rios, only 3 hours from Buenos Aires' international airport, and is therefore ideal for residents and visitors alike who have tight schedules, want to avoid flying, or are simply looking for a quick escape from the city.

Pica Zuro, Cordoba Province

Contact: Rob McAndrew – rmcandrew@argentinaoutfitters.com

This dove lodge is a tasteful facility that operates in hotel fashion and offers high-volume dove hunts organized by well-known outfitter David Denies.

DUCK-SHOOTING

Estancia Ameghino, Florentino Ameghino, Buenos Aires Province
Contact: Rob McAndrew – rmcandrew@argentinaoutfitters.com

This typically Argentine *estancia* lies in the heart of duck country, near Ameghino, north of Buenos Aires. Situated within the largest grain-producing area of Argentina, this region is the best-kept secret for waterfowl-shooting. The surrounding areas support a wide variety of duck species, guaranteeing a great mixed-bag hunt, as well as being a perfect setting for experiencing superb decoyed duck shooting.

Estancia La Calera, Gualeguay, Entre Rios Province
Contact: Rob McAndrew – rmcandrew@argentinaoutfitters.com

Located in Entre Rios, La Calera is only a three-hour drive from Buenos Aires international airport. This delta region is renowned for the large numbers of ducks it holds year after year, allowing clients to enjoy duck hunts in the grand Argentine style. One great bonus of hunting here is how easy it is to reach the duck-hunting areas, almost all of which are conveniently located on the ranch's private property.

Tata Inti Lodge, Merlo, San Luis Province
Contact: Rob McAndrew – rmcandrew@argentinaoutfitters.com

Tata is one of the country's top destinations for high-volume dove, decoyed pigeon and *perdiz* (partridge) shooting. The friendly lodge offers a unique mountain-shooting environment with a comfortable microclimate.

RED STAG HUNTING

Lago Hermoso, San Martin de los Andes, Neuquen Province
Contact: Patrick Steverlynck – ps@argentinaoutfitters.com

This beautiful mountain property, just 23 miles south of San Martin de los Andes, covers some 14,000 acres of Lanin National Park, offering an incomparable hunting experience in the rugged mountains surrounding the stunning Lago Hermoso.

WILD BOAR HUNTING

Los Araucanos Lodge, General Acha, La Pampa Province
Contact: Patrick Steverlynck – ps@argentinaoutfitters.com

This 46,000-acre private ranch encompasses a varied landscape of grassy plains, sand dunes, creeks and woodlands, providing the ideal conditions for several big-game species as well as for wing-shooting. Species hunted all year round include Russian boar, black buck antelope and puma, while red stag can be hunted from March to May. One of the unique aspects of Los Araucanos is the African safari-style camp overlooking a picturesque lagoon, which combines luxurious comfort with the experience of being in the heart of the Argentine outback.

IGUAZU FALLS

Las Taguas, Carlos Pellegrini 113, Buenos Aires
Tel: 5032 0042 www.lastaguas.com

The impressive Iguazu Falls, at 269 feet, are higher than the Niagara Falls and twice as wide, with 275 cascades spread out in a horseshoe over almost two miles of the Iguazu river. These falls were created by a volcanic eruption that left a crack in the earth. During the rainy season (from November to March), 450,000 cubic feet of water fall per second. If you don't have time to stay overnight at the Sheraton Hotel (see Sleep), then definitely opt for the day trip – a private flight leaves from Buenos Aires.

POLO

Campo Argentino de Polo, Avenida del Libertador 4300, Recoleta
Tel: 4777 6444 www.aapolo.com
Tickets from www.ticketek.com.ar (tel: 5237 7200)

The 'cathedral of polo', or just 'Palermo' as it is known to those in the game, is the Lord's Cricket Ground, the Wembley or the Shea Stadium of polo. The Argentine Open is played here from November through to mid-December and is unquestionably the greatest polo tournament on earth. Whereas 26-goal polo is the maximum handicapped tournament outside of Argentina, the Argentine Open can include teams of up to 40 goals, which is the maximum possible handicap that a team can have (each of the four players on a team has a maximum handicap of 10 goals). Eight teams, all of which have around 40 horses between them, play for the Argentine Open, which is the third of the season's Triple Crown tournaments (the first is the Tortugas Open, the second the Hurlingham).

Centauros, Avenida Vcio Castro 1400, Pilar
Tel: 02322 431 837

Centauros continues to draw in the world's top players, and is still accessible if you have the cash to play ball.

Coronel Suarez Polo Club, Seccion Quintas 7540, Coronel Suarez
Tel: 02926 422 547

A four-hour drive south of Buenos Aires, Coronel Suarez is perhaps the home of polo in Argentina. The Araya and Harriot families are among several of renown that reside in the area.

Ellerstina Polo Club, Rodriguez
Buenos Aires office: Cerrito 1266 6° 26
Tel. 4813 9241   www.ellerstina.com.ar

Kerry Packer ploughed money into Pilar Chico and the Pieres family have continued to ensure that this is one of the top clubs in the game. The Ellerstina High Goal team narrowly missed out on the Triple Crown in 2005, but continues to play some of the fastest polo of the modern game.

El Molino Viejo
Tel: 02227 1553 8190 www.polomolinoviejo.com.ar / eamaya@pololine.com

Eduardo Amaya is one of Argentina's top polo teachers, perhaps the best. Aside from being a vet, he has played polo in four continents as a professional. Father of four, two of whom are professional polo players (Sebastian Amaya runs www.pololine.com), Eduardo has his own breed of horses, and has just expanded his operation with a new ground. You can either stay at the ranch for a few days or travel down to Lobos for the day. If there is a glitch in your swing, Eduardo will take it apart, reconstruct it and make it work.

Puesto Viejo, Ruta 6, Cañuelas
Tel: 15 5185 5424/1667 www.puestoviejo.com

Marcial Socas could well be the most relaxed man in Argentina. His half-brother, Adolfo Cambiasso, is the best polo player on the planet (although Bautista Heguy would disagree). His wife, Joanna, makes rawhide handbags for Harrods, while Marcial has an army of grooms who look after his horses. This leaves him time to teach guests how to play polo. Whereas Eduardo Amaya is hands-on and technical, Marcial's approach is more relaxed ('Just hit a few and we'll have a chat about how you can improve'). If you want to try out polo, this is the man to ease you into it. If you already know how to play, then he will call in some frighteningly good players to up the standard of play. The Puesto Viejo farm is an hour's drive from the city, and lunch will be waiting for you when you arrive. There are 10 guest rooms at the farm for those wanting the full Argentine polo experience.

Polo Connection, Opendoor, Lujan
Tel: 15 4536 1451 www.poloconnection.com

Kevin Greenleaves and Pepe Gallardo run this polo school in Opendoor, right beside the Novillo Astrada family's La Aguada farm (La Aguada won the Argentine Open and the Triple Crown – the big three high goal tournaments of the Argentine season – in 2003). The horses are all of high quality and the chukkas are all medium goal and above. It's a charming place to come and play. Pepe gives the lessons, while Carolina runs the guesthouse, which faces the swimming pool and polo pitch. It's ideal for a day trip or for a couple of days' stay.

RUGBY

The Pumas (Argentina's national team) have been climbing the world rankings for the last decade and there is now a suggestion they are ready to join what is at the moment the Tri-Nations competition involving the All Blacks (New Zealand), the Wallabies (Australia) and the Springboks (South Africa).

Like football, rugby union was introduced to Argentina by the British in 1873, and the Argentine rugby union (UAR) (www.uar.com.ar) was formed in 1899. In Buenos Aires, internationals are either played at the River Plate stadium (www.cariverplate.com.ar) or the Velez Sarsfield stadium (www.velezsarsfield.com.ar). For tickets try the UAR website or Ticketek (www.ticketek.com.ar). For club rugby in Argentina the two leading exponents are Club Athletico de San Isidro (CASI) and San Isidro Club (SIC).

Club Athletico de San Isidro, Roque Saenz Pena 499, San Isidro
Tel: 4743 4242 www.casi.org.ar

San Isidro Club, Blanco Encalada 404, San Isidro
Tel: 4776 2030 / 4763 2039 www.sanisidroclub.com.ar

SAILING

El Catalejo Sailing, Alicia Moreau de Justo 1180, Office 408 C, Puerto Madero
Tel: 15 4162 7795

Either take a 45-foot yacht out from Puerto Madero and sail down the River Plate (capacity for seven guests), or be picked up from your hotel and be taken to the Tigre delta, where a 36-foot yacht will cruise up the waterways. Lunch is provided, or you can visit Club Europeo for an afternoon snack before heading back to the city.

SALTA

Las Taguas, Carlos Pellegrini 1135, Buenos Aires
Tel: +5411 5032 0042 www.lastaguas.com

Bolivia, Chile and Paraguay, as well as six other Argentine provinces, border the northwestern province of Salta. The city itself was founded in 1582, and the towns and villages are not only fine examples of Spanish colonial architecture but also bear witness to their Diaguita–Calchaqui and Inca heritage.

The first people to live here called the area 'Sagta', which in the Aymara language means 'the very beautiful one'. Salta is a stunning part of Argentina to visit. The Calchaqui valleys are famous for their vineyards and their breathtaking multi-coloured rock formations. After the glaciers and the Iguazu falls, Salta should be third on your list. The House of Jasmines is the best hotel in the area (see Sleep).

SPAS

Aqua Vita Medical Spa, Arenales 1965, Recoleta

Tel: 4812 5989 www.aquavitamedicalspa.com
Open: daily, 9am–9pm

Well located in Recoleta, Aqua Vita Medical Spa is the first of its kind in BA, combining hydrotherapy with a variety of aesthetic treatments. Dr Ruben Muhlberger, who specializes in anti-ageing therapies, leads the team. On the menu are anti-stress days, beauty days, most kinds of massage and treatments such as breast and buttock firming and electro-lifting facials.

Evian Agua Club Spa, Cerviño 3626, Palermo

Tel: 4807 4688 www.aguaclubspa.com
Open: 7.30am–10.30pm Mon–Fri; 10am–9pm Sat–Sun

The Evian is well known among stressed, wealthy locals looking to unwind from the soul-sapping daily life of Buenos Aires. It's more commercial and less technical than the Aqua Vita spa, which seems to make it more attractive to men. This spa has a long list of massages, so if it's a rub down and a Finnish bath you are after, the Evian Agua Club Spa is the one for you.

SKIING

Las Taguas, Carlos Pellegrini, Buenos Aires

Tel: 5032 0042 www.lastaguas.com

Argentina has three main ski resorts in Patagonia and one in Tierra del Fuego. Bariloche is now the most advanced – having amalgamated two sides of its mountain, while San Martin de Los Andes and Las Leñas are on a par in terms of lengths of pistes (although Las Leñas is more challenging in parts). We recommend you go to Bariloche, which is the largest ski resorts in South America. The ski season begins in July and can go on until as late as September.

SKY-DIVING

Paracaidismo Lobos
Tel: 02227 15 53 9027; 15 5120 4131 (courses); 15 4421 3250 (tandems)
www.paracaidismolobos.com.ar

Lobos is the most important drop zone in Argentina and is only 65 miles south of Buenos Aires; here you can jump out of a plane over the vast expanse of Pampa plains. Why not make a jump in the morning before heading off for a couple of chukkas of polo in the afternoon? Now, that's hedonism.

TIERRA DEL FUEGO

Las Taguas, Carlos Pellegrini, Buenos Aires
Tel: +5411 5032 0042 www.lastaguas.com

In three and a half hours from Buenos Aires you can be at the end of the world. Tierra del Fuego, which means 'Land of Fire', is a 28,476 square mile archipelago separated from the southernmost tip of South American mainland by the Strait of Magellan (Ferdinand Magellan was the first European to navigate the strait in 1520). The tip of Tierra del Fuego is also known as Cape Horn, famous for claiming many a sailor's life. The primitive inhabitants of Tierra del Fuego were the Yamanas. In 1830, Robert Fitzroy took four natives of the area back to the King and Queen in England, where they became famous. Charles Darwin later returned to the islands on the Beagle. Tierra del Fuego is a must-see for the complete Argentina experience. Consider popping down to Ushuaia after a trip to the glacier.

Wake School, Tigre Delta
Tel: 4728 0031 or 15 4414 5129 (cell) www.wakeschool.com.ar

Gabriela Diaz is a 10-time national champion, three-time South American Champion and runner-up in the wakeboarding world championship. It follows, then, that she's the girl to take you wakeboarding. There is also wakeboarding at La Pascuala Delta Lodge (see Sleep).

Mendoza Wine tours
Tel: +5411 6621 0661 www.fueguito.com

Mendoza is the home of wine in Argentina, and it is only a quick flight over the pampas plains to the foothills of the Andes, where the vineyards stretch for miles. English-born Katherine Pottinger will organize the most exclusive wine tour of Mendoza. Luckily she will also cater to your needs and budget. She has access to all of the vineyards in the area, so contact her to arrange your trip (including accommodation and flights).

Terroir Casa de Vinos, Buschiazzo 3040, Palermo
Tel: 4778 3443/3408 www.terroir.com.ar

Argentine wine has become more and more renowned for its taste over the last decade. The country is now famous for both its Malbec and Torrontes wines. Tastings at Terroir, just two blocks away from the American embassy, can be an excellent warm-up to shipping a few cases home. Terroir are one of the most reliable shippers of wine, so rest assured that any tax and customs issues will be resolved before you have had one glass too many.

For further advice on buying wine try Luciano Sosto (Former President of Argentine Sommeliers) Tel: 4802 1262 or 15 4070 6934 (cell), luckyuino@fibertel.com.

info...

APPEARANCE

Argentine men take a lot of care in their appearance. The Argentine man is now metrosexual. Looking cool is more about attitude in Buenos Aires than anything else, but a stylish pair of jeans, a slightly muscle-hugging but rock-star T-shirt and a slick pair of sneakers are the basics of an Argentine's wardrobe. A little stubble is okay, too much frightens the girls off. Sunglasses are advisable. Foreign girls start with the huge disadvantage of actually having eaten properly over the last decade. Argentine girls are skinny and little, but do not be intimidated by their perfect figures – having spent years sipping on *mate* (green tea drunk through a straw) and diet coke, and churning through 20 Marlboros a day, they have paid a price.

DRUGS

First off, we'd like to point out drugs are illegal in Argentina. Although, ecstasy and cocaine are prevalent in Buenos Aires, ketamine has made a surge in recent years, and marijuana, as in most cities, is widely available. Rave clubs and after-hours clubs are full of narcotics. If you do want to buy drugs, there are plenty of dealers in the large clubs as well as in the 'afters', and it's just a case of asking who is selling. Just be careful and know what you're buying/taking.

GETTING IN

The velvet ropes in Buenos Aires are easy to cross if you know the right people or if you turn up with pretty girls. We don't want you to have to wait in any queue, so you'll need to take a note of the following information: visit Moi Altuna's website: www.moialtuna.com, or call: 15 4917 8000 or 6349 6149 for Asia de Cuba, Araoz and Crobar. Otherwise contact Sangre Travel Design, who, in addition to offering an extensive concierge service, will arrange for you to get into any club's VIP section for a small fee: 4805 2584 / 15 5469 3450 (cell) or angiecortesi@gmail.com

MONEY

In 2002 the Argentine peso (AR$) was devalued after a decade of being pegged to the dollar. After an initial drop the currency has since stabilised at a rate of US$–AR$3, €1–AR$4, £1–AR$6. Most places take credit cards and there are plenty of ATMs on the street. Always check your change and look out for forged notes.

SECURITY

Because of the country's troubled past, Buenos Aires has a dog-eat-dog culture, and the crime rate here has always been a concern. However, if you are sensible you should be fine. Count your change, lock your taxi cab door, keep your phone in your pocket, do not leave your bag on a table and try to blend in. Buenos Aires has its ugly side, but this is easily avoided if you're careful. Try not to be alone in ATM booths and don't take taxis waiting directly outside banks.

TAXIS

Argentine taxi drivers drive the equivalent of twice around the world annually. There are 40,000 taxis in town. All taxi drivers are canny, and all know the city better than they would have you think, so look on a map before you set out, buckle up, pay attention to how many circles they are taking you in and check how many forged notes they give you in change. Always carry less than a AR$50 peso note. Favour the cabs with Radio Taxi signs and *aire condicionado* plaques.

TELEPHONES

All landline numbers in Buenos Aires consist of eight digits and begin with 4 or 5. Mobile phones begin with 15. If calling a landline from abroad, dial 0054 11 before the landline number, and dial 0054 911 and take off the 15 for a mobile number.

WEATHER

Temperatures range from 35° Celsius (95° Fahrenheit) in January to 10° Celsius (50° Fahrenheit) in July. The best months to come are from September to December, when the flowering jacaranda trees paint the city purple and the weather begins to heat up. Summer is the most popular season for tourism and it's the perfect time to go to Patagonia and Argentina's colder regions. During the autumn the weather is mild, and it's still a pleasant time to visit. Although it has snowed only once in Buenos Aires' history, winters are chilly and wet, but nothing in comparison to those that Europeans are used to.